DATE DUE

NO 27 '19			
			PRINTED IN U.S.A.

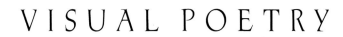

VISUAL POETRY

VISUAL

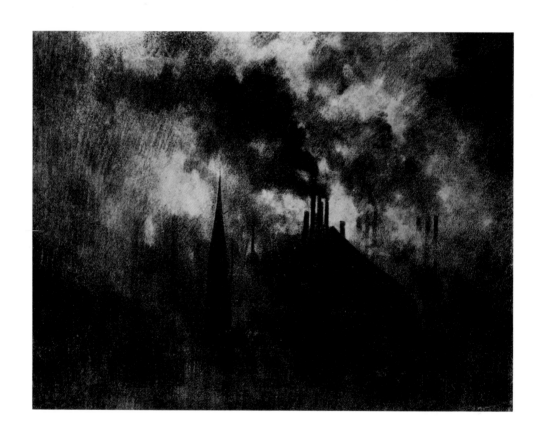

POETRY

The Drawings of Joseph Stella

Joann Moser

Published for the National Museum of American Art

by the Smithsonian Institution Press   Washington and London

Riverside Community College
APR '14 Library
4800 Magnolia Avenue
Riverside, CA 92506

N6537.S73 A4 1990
Stella, Joseph, 1877-1946.
Visual poetry : the drawin
of Joseph Stella

...sion of the exhibition
...awings of Joseph Stella,
organized by the ...ional Museum of American
Art, Smithsonian Institution, and The Amon
Carter Museum

Amon Carter Museum, Fort Worth, Texas
23 February–22 April 1990

Museum of Fine Arts, Boston
19 May–22 July 1990

National Museum of American Art
Smithsonian Institution, Washington, D.C.
7 September–12 November 1990

© 1990 by Smithsonian Institution. All rights
reserved. No part of this publication may be
reproduced in any form without the prior
permission of the Smithsonian Institution Press
and the National Museum of American Art,
Smithsonian Institution, Washington, D.C.

Edited by Terence Winch
Designed by Lisa Buck Vann
Typeset by Monotype Composition, Baltimore
Printed by Toppan Printing Company, Ltd., Japan

Library of Congress Cataloging-in-Publication Data
Stella, Joseph, 1877-1946.
Visual poetry.
Catalog of an exhibition held at the Amon Carter
Museum, Ft. Worth, Tex., Feb. 23–Apr. 22, 1990;
Museum of Fine Arts, Boston, May 19–Jul. 22,
1990; and the National Museum of American Art,
Smithsonian Institution, Washington, D.C.,
Sept. 7–Nov. 12, 1990.
Bibliography: p.
Includes index.
I. Stella, Joseph, 1877-1946—Exhibitions.
I. Moser, Joann.
II. Amon Carter Museum of Western Art.
III. Museum of Fine Arts Boston.
IV. National Museum of American Art (U.S.)
V. Title.
N6537.S73A4   1990   741.973   89-11520
ISBN 0-87474-738-4 (cloth)
ISBN 0-87474-731-7 (pbk)

All works are on paper unless otherwise specified.
Front Cover: *Purple Waterlilies* (detail), 1944.
Private collection (see fig. 114).
Back Cover: *Red Pepper*, 1944 (see fig. 130).
Frontispiece: *Chimneys, Pittsburgh*, ca. 1908 (see fig. 53).
The paper used in this publication meets the
requirements of the American National Standard
for Permanence of Paper for Printed Library
Materials Z39.48-1984.

CONTENTS

FOREWORD

Joseph Stella was at once one of the most innovative and traditional of American modernist artists in the early years of this century. No matter how energetically he reached for the future, he kept one hand firmly on the past. His subjects ranged from Pittsburgh smokestacks and Coney Island to Italian peasants and the song of the nightingale, and his aesthetic repertoire included a chromatic variant of Futurism, collaged abstractions that echo Cubism, and metalpoint drawings in the Renaissance manner. Stella processed into art everything in his path, from the emerging industrial city and its immigrants to the worlds of nature and music to the intimacy of a sleeping figure. To render such variety, he mastered a dazzling array of techniques and styles, and his virtuosity at matching each subject to an expressive idiom was equaled by few artists of his time.

Stella's drawings represent a vital component of American modernism. Their enormous number, from which the sixty images in this exhibition were selected, reveals an appetite for experience and sensation, perception and symbolism that is the hallmark of a restless, far-ranging intellectual curiosity. Rather than developing his drawings as a straightforward stylistic progression, Stella chose a sequence of detours and doublings-back that might appear almost directionless. This method of working, reworking, and reexamining, however, ultimately led him to an unparalleled knowledge of his art and craft.

In his belief that art was an appropriate tool for examining a variety of life forms, Stella perpetuated a Renaissance attitude begun with Leonardo and Dürer. His sensitive observation of social types and physiognomies continued a long artistic tradition. He also gave poignant voice to the emotions of American immigrants, whose transition from old world to new was an experience that Stella, himself an immigrant, knew firsthand.

Joseph Stella retained old hierarchies and formulas for the creation of art and believed that major paintings were composed through a long process of intuitive assimilation. While his contemporaries often worked out their ideas directly on canvas, without benefit of preparatory drawings, Stella saw his drawings as the proper forum for minute observation, sensory experience, and experimentation. His drawings not only present the subjects for his paintings in different media but provide deeper insight into the artist's complex personality.

The curator for this exhibition is Joann Moser, curator-in-charge of graphic arts at the National Museum of American Art. Supported by a Smithsonian Scholarly Studies Grant, Dr. Moser undertook the enormous but rewarding task of reviewing Stella's graphic oeuvre to select the exhibition drawings. Her essay reveals the multivalent connections found throughout his work, and her deep knowledge of Stella's art provides many fresh insights.

The Amon Carter Museum and the National Museum of American Art are pleased to collaborate on this exhibition. The Amon Carter Museum staff handled its organization, while the NMAA publications office oversaw the preparation of this book and the Smithsonian Institution Press produced it.

The exhibition would not have been possible without the generous cooperation of the many lenders. Finally, both museums are deeply grateful to the National Endowment for the Arts for providing vital support.

Elizabeth Broun
Director
National Museum of American Art
Washington, D.C.

Jan Keene Muhlert
Director
Amon Carter Museum
Fort Worth, Texas

ACKNOWLEDGMENTS

One of the most rewarding aspects of studying the drawings of Joseph Stella has been the opportunity to look at and discuss the works with three people who knew the artist and who could speak of him and his art from personal experience. Sergio Stella, Joseph Stella's nephew, with whom the artist had become especially close during his last years, made available for my perusal a large number of drawings that he had inherited directly from his uncle. His fond memories gave the artist a human dimension from which insights into his art could proceed. Similarly, Bernard

Rabin, the surviving member of Rabin and Krueger, Stella's gallery during the last decade of his life, made available to me hundreds of drawings and incidental sketches that had remained in the gallery's inventory. If any artist may be considered Stella's protégé in his later years, it was certainly August Mosca, who generously shared his reminiscences and observations from a fellow artist's point of view.

This publication represents the culmination of more than six years' study of Joseph Stella's drawings, much of which time was spent finding and seeing as many works as possible. This search was aided immeasurably by the many art dealers who have handled works by Joseph Stella and who most generously furnished photographs of works they had sold, often putting me in touch with many of the purchasers. I would especially like to thank Richard York and Bob and Jane Schoelkopf for the numerous hours they spent showing me drawings, tracking collectors, sharing insights, and encouraging my progress. Because I could not travel to see every drawing that I had located, I am indebted to everyone who helped me obtain photographs of works for consideration, especially Amy Worthen and the Donald Morris Gallery.

The most rewarding moments in the research process were those when I had the opportunity to discover and see a drawing for the first time, often in the homes of collectors. Without naming each individually, I would like to express my sincere appreciation for their cooperation in opening their homes to me and sharing their enthusiasm for Stella's work. I am equally grateful to colleagues in the many museums around the country who showed me the drawings by Joseph Stella in their collections and assisted me in obtaining photographs. Word of mouth was an important tool for locating additional works of art, and I would like to thank everyone whose mention of my project resulted in the discovery of new drawings.

At times the process of studying Stella's drawings was less a matter of finding documentation than of exchanging observations and ideas with colleagues whose interests and expertise complemented and expanded my own. The original impetus for my study of Stella's drawings was a casual conversation with Jane Glaubinger, whose interest and enthusiasm continued to be encouraging throughout the research phase of this project. Discussions with Ruth Bohan, Wanda Corn, Judith Zilczer, Charles Eldredge, and Noel Frackman on specific aspects of Stella's work provided enlightening insights into the subject. My sincere appreciation goes to Barbara Wolanin, Greta Berman,

Elizabeth Broun, Jan Muhlert, and Jane Myers for their comments on a draft of my manuscript that helped greatly in writing the final version of my essay. I am particularly grateful to our staff editor Terence Winch for his careful attention to this book.

Moyra Byrne provided careful and sensitive translations from Italian of Stella's writings that had not already been translated in Irma Jaffe's book on Stella. I would also like to thank Timothy Vitale and Maria Alexiou, conservators at the Smithsonian's Conservation Analytical Laboratory, for their attempt to determine by X-ray fluorescence the metals used in several of Stella's drawings. Fern Bleckner and Catherine Maynor, paper conservators at the National Museum of American Art, were most helpful with questions concerning technique or preservation. To the staff members of the Graphic Arts Department of the NMAA goes my appreciation for their understanding when my work on this project took precedence over all other concerns.

I am grateful to Brenda Palley for her tireless and dedicated help in the early stages of my research, tracking down drawings, assembling the bibliography, and searching archives and libraries for information on Stella's life and art. David Gallalee's skillful collating of information relating to Stella's drawings reproduced in *The Survey* magazine greatly aided the progress of my understanding of the artist's work as an illustrator. In the latter stages of my research and writing, Diane Tepfer's help in compiling the chronology and captions, contacting owners of the works illustrated, checking sources and information, ordering photographs, and performing a myriad of other indispensable tasks was essential for the timely completion of this project. I would also like to thank Molly Donovan, Katharine Stewart, and Neal Kobayashi for their invaluable assistance with the intricacies of word processing and computer hardware.

This publication was written in conjunction with an exhibition of Joseph Stella's drawings, cosponsored by the Amon Carter Museum and the National Museum of American Art. I would like to thank Jan Keene Muhlert, director of the Amon Carter Museum, for her continuing support of this project since its inception. The suggestions, reactions, and enthusiasm of Linda Ayres, formerly curator of the Amon Carter Museum, and Jane Myers, associate curator of the museum, were most helpful. The interest and encouragement of Charles Eldredge, former director of the National Museum of American Art, and Elizabeth Broun, director of the museum, were essential to the realization of this exhibition and book. I am grateful for a grant toward the publication of this book from the Lachaise Foundation, Boston. Much of my research on Joseph Stella's drawings was made possible by a Scholarly Studies Grant from the Smithsonian Institution.

Finally, I would like to express my appreciation to my husband, Nicholas Berkoff, and daughter, Alexandra, for the many evenings and weekends when they had to compete with Joseph Stella for my attention.

JM

PREFACE

Joseph Stella has been acclaimed as America's most important Futurist artist. His 1919 painting *Brooklyn Bridge* has become an icon of American modernism, and his subsequent interpretations of this subject have even more firmly linked Stella's reputation with this image. His early career fits a pattern common to several leading artists of his generation. Born in Italy, he immigrated to the United States as a young man, settled in New York City, and received his early art training at one of the leading art schools. He did illustrations to support himself, focusing on his urban surroundings for subject matter. After visiting Europe during a period of intense artistic ferment from 1910 through 1912, Stella brought back to New York some of the most advanced ideas being explored by the most innovative artists of the day. He participated in the ground-breaking Armory Show of 1913 and shortly afterward painted and exhibited *Battle of Lights, Coney Island*, a major, controversial painting that clearly identified him as one of the leading exponents of some of the most radical ideas in art of that time. By the 1920s he had achieved critical acclaim and financial success beyond that of many of his contemporaries.

At the height of his recognition, the momentum of Stella's development toward abstraction seemed to come to an abrupt halt. Several of his later paintings refer back to the Futurist style on which his reputation was built, but most of his work of the next twenty-five years, until his death in 1946, side-stepped the mainstream of contemporary art. In contrast to the urban realism, regionalism, or modernist abstraction that characterized most American art during the period between the two world wars, Stella's paintings and works on paper ranged from religious themes and decorative, symbolic compositions to landscapes, still lifes, and a few portraits. Out of step with the march toward modernism, his reputation declined, and he spent his last years away from the public eye, but no less committed to his singular vision than he had been throughout his life.

In their monographs of 1970 and 1971, Irma Jaffe and John I. H. Baur went a long way toward reconstructing the events and developments of Stella's career and fostering an appreciation of the artist. Many critics and art historians, however, have neglected to consider seriously any aspect of his work other than his most famous Futurist paintings.

Meanwhile, our historical perspective has changed and our understanding of modernism has broadened. The emphasis on formalist analysis and stylistic innovation that has dominated art history and criticism since the 1950s is being questioned by those who seek to understand the content of the work of art and the cultural context in which it was created. The tendency to classify and pigeonhole an artist as a member of a particular movement or group is giving way to a more sympathetic consideration of the artist as an individual. A more fluid understanding of relationships, influences, and motivations has replaced the more linear interpretation of successive art movements in which progress toward modernism eclipsed other considerations.

Stella's works on paper furnish some insights into the romantic, symbolist, and mystical aspects of his creative expression. The visual language with which Stella expressed himself over the course of his career varied dramatically. The stylistic inconsistencies that characterize his work, even within a single year, testify to his constant exploration of expressive devices, which he used to infuse the material world with spiritual significance and to create a symbolic language of form to express his personal fantasies, visions, and dreams.

Recent scholarship has shown these concerns to be more prevalent among the leading modernist artists than had previously been acknowledged.[1] As Linda Henderson has astutely proposed in her introduction to a recent article on mysticism and occultism in modern art: "No longer can we accept a streamlined, secularized history of modernism that presents modern art as a product of those attitudes towards reality which characterize the historian's own milieu rather than that of the late nineteenth or early twentieth century."[2]

Joseph Stella dedicated his life to art and found inspiration as much in poetry and music as he did in the visual arts. Some of his imagery has more in common with William Carlos Williams and Hart Crane than it does with his fellow visual artists. Openly acknowledging his admiration for Dante, Shakespeare, Thoreau, Whitman, and Poe, Stella found inspiration as well in the poetry of Baudelaire and Mallarmé. The exuberance of his prose, as well as the dramatic, mystical imagery that typifies much of his writing, reveals an artist who conceived his art as visual poetry.

Developments in recent years have suggested a new perspective with which to view the art of the past. Drawing, for example, has emerged in the 1970s and 1980s as an independent means of expression, at times on a scale of importance comparable to an artist's paintings or sculptures. The increasing visibility of drawings as independent works of art has encouraged reconsideration of drawings by earlier artists, not only as a look at an artist's work in another medium, but more importantly as a body of work that might be judged on its own merit and that might reveal aspects of an artist's personality or stylistic development that are less apparent in more public or finished works. It is with such a premise that this study of Joseph Stella's drawings has been undertaken. Their extraordinary quality has been recognized by art historians and critics almost without exception. Stella has been called "one of the outstanding draftsmen in the history of American art."[3]

For the purpose of this study, the term "drawing" has been interpreted to include all of Stella's works on paper, including his watercolors, pastels, and collages. Relatively few individual drawings were given titles by Stella, and the titles now associated with these works are usually descriptive, assigned by art dealers or owners of the works. As interesting as it would be to know the exact sequence of Stella's interests and stylistic development, it is almost impossible to date most of Stella's drawings with any certainty. Many sheets are undated and the dates on others are unreliable. Stella was known to have signed numerous works many years after they were completed, often adding a second signature to a work already signed. Hence, it might be assumed that he also dated some works long after they were completed. Because he worked in several styles and media simultaneously, stylistic similarities are not always a reliable indication of date. Furthermore, he revived earlier styles and subjects in his later work. Illustrated catalogues and articles published during his lifetime help date some works, but his unpublished writings are undated for the most part and provide little information about the chronology of his stylistic development. Despite the difficulty of establishing a precise chronological progression of Stella's drawings, it is possible to explore his interests and motivations at various stages in his career and to understand how his drawings functioned as important touchstones for his creative explorations.

Joann Moser
Curator-in-Charge, Graphic Arts
National Museum of American Art

1. See *The Spiritual in Art: Abstract Painting, 1890–1985* (Los Angeles: Los Angeles County Museum of Art, 1986).

2. "Editor's Statement: Mysticism and Occultism in Modern Art," *Art Journal* 46, no. 1 (Spring 1987): 6.

3. Barbara Rose, *American Art Since 1900* (New York: Frederick A. Praeger, Inc., 1968), p. 106.

VISUAL POETRY

The Drawings of Joseph Stella

Although recognized as one of the leading early modernist artists in America, Joseph Stella is known primarily for a small group of his major paintings. A prolific and masterful draftsman as well, Stella made thousands of drawings throughout his entire career. The scope and diversity of his drawings reveal the creative processes, poetic imagination, careful observations, humanistic concerns, sense of humor, and private passions of a complex artist. Working on paper with a broad range of materials, Stella created a large body of work that shows him to be one of the most sensitive and versatile draftsmen of the twentieth century.

His drawings enhance our understanding of the conflicts, tensions, and ambivalence that characterized many aspects of his life and artistic creation. Many drawings are no more than quick sketches, informal notes from his daily experiences, while others are fully developed compositions of a scale and importance comparable to his paintings. The sheer quantity of Stella's works on paper suggests that drawing was a constant activity, even during periods when he made very few paintings.

The Young Artist

The Stellas were among the better educated and relatively prosperous families in Muro Lucano, the medieval mountain town in the southern Italian region of Basilicata near Naples where Joseph Stella was born. Like his four brothers, Joseph enjoyed a classical education in preparation for a professional career, receiving a diploma, probably from the same school in Naples that his brother Antonio had attended. Joseph Stella arrived in New York in March 1896, a young man of eighteen. His father and brothers had preceded him to America, and the eldest brother, Antonio, already a prominent physician and leader in Italian-American affairs in New York, seems to have assumed primary responsibility for his younger brother. Doubtless at the urging of Antonio, Joseph began to study medicine and pharmacology shortly after landing in America.

In 1897 he abandoned his medical studies and enrolled in the Art Students League. According to his later reminiscences, his discovery of art came as a young boy, but he kept this passion to himself, a private source of joy and inspiration.[1] Stella seems to have had an early and natural talent for drawing that he developed with little formal training. He made sketches of his friends and classmates in Italy, and a few sheets remain from his childhood and youth.[2] Stella continued to paint and sketch after he came to New York, for within a year or two of his arrival, he had work to show Carlo de Fornaro, an acquaintance of Antonio's with training as an artist, who assured Antonio that his younger brother had talent and deserved a chance to develop it.[3] Joseph convinced Antonio to support him while he studied art.

Stella attended the Art Students League for only a few months.[4] An interview published in the New York *Sun* (25 May 1913) suggested one of the possible reasons for his brief enrollment: "One of the objections young

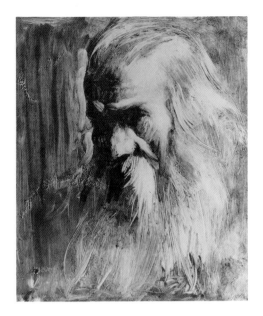 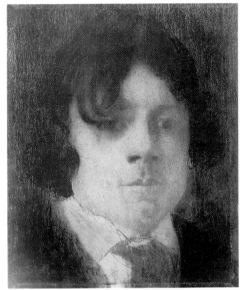

Figure 1

Untitled (Bearded old man)
Monotype in brown ink
13 x 11½ in.
Private Collection

Figure 2

Portrait of a Young Man,
ca. 1909–10
Crayon, oil, and varnish
on paper mounted on
paperboard
12 x 9¾ in.
National Museum of
American Art,
Smithsonian Institution
Washington, D.C.

Stella had to the professors' teaching was a rule forbidding the pupils to paint flowers."[5] More than an amusing anecdote that illustrates Stella's continuing delight in drawing and painting flowers, this statement reveals early dissatisfaction with what Stella perceived to be academic rigidity and arbitrary rules.

Shortly afterward, probably in 1898, Stella enrolled in the New York School of Art, headed by the international celebrity and popular teacher William Merritt Chase, who had left the Art Students League in 1896 to start his own school.[6] In contrast to the more traditional structure of the Art Students League, there were no qualification tests for admission, and anyone familiar with the elements of drawing was allowed to enroll in the painting class. Drawing was taught simultaneously with color. Instead of drawing from plaster casts, beginning students were allowed to start working immediately from life, a practice traditionally reserved for advanced students.

Chase's direct influence is most apparent in some of Stella's early paintings. Stella's use of a heavily loaded brush and method of modeling in light and shadow with quick strokes of paint recall his teacher's painting techniques. Several early monotypes by Stella exhibit the painterly manipulation of tone and spontaneous gesture characteristic of Chase's own monotypes (fig. 1). An oil sketch of a young man, executed in crayon and oil on paper covered with varnish (fig. 2), recalls his teacher's prolific use of oil sketches, while the pose and expression are reminiscent of such portraits as Chase's painting of his daughter, *Head of a Girl* (ca. 1899; North Carolina Museum of

Art, Raleigh). It is possible that Chase's celebrated work in the pastel medium influenced Stella's own lifelong involvement with pastels, even though the two artists' work in the medium was quite different. At his summer school in Shinnecock Hills, Long Island, which Stella attended in 1901, Chase encouraged his students to draw and paint outdoors. By the end of that summer Stella had so completely mastered Chase's style of figure painting that one of his portrait studies earned him Chase's compliment that "Manet couldn't have done it better!" and a round of applause from his fellow students.[7]

Because of Stella's reputation as a modernist and Chase's well-known disdain for modern art, the long-term impact of his teaching on Stella's subsequent development is not obvious. Many of the attitudes and values that Chase instilled in his students, however, seem to have influenced Stella throughout his career. Chase fostered independence and individuality by encouraging his students to leave school once they had mastered the basic techniques with which to express themselves. He urged his students to visit art museums and examine carefully the paintings of the Old Masters, to look at contemporary paintings in exhibitions and art magazines, and to study reproductions of masterpieces for the purpose of stimulation rather than critical analysis. Although it was acceptable to emulate another artist whose work one admired, Chase insisted that his students not work slavishly in the manner of any one artist but combine the best of what they saw in the work of many artists. He encouraged experimentation and valued inspiration over order and method. He taught that the task of the true artist was to transform a mundane subject into a work of art.[8]

Eschewing the literary, moralistic, and idealistic traditions of the nineteenth century, Chase transmitted the "art for art's sake" attitude that he shared with his friend James McNeill Whistler. Stella was not the only modernist artist to have studied with Chase; Georgia O'Keeffe, Arthur B. Carles, Charles Sheeler, Patrick Henry Bruce, Charles Demuth, Alfred Maurer, and others benefited during their formative years from the solid foundation in technique that Chase had given them, as well as from his emphasis on inspiration as the source of creative expression.

The Old Master Tradition

Following Chase's admonition to study the masterpieces of the past, Stella frequented the Metropolitan Museum of Art, where he was able to see work

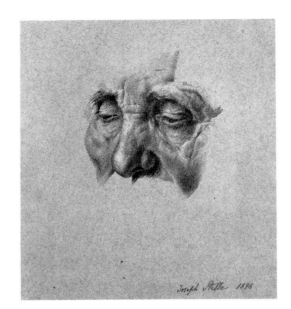

Figure 3

Old Man, ca. 1898
Pen and brown ink on
brown paper
8½ x 8⅛ in.
Collection, The Museum
of Modern Art, New
York

by some of the artists his teacher most admired. Rather than limit himself to
a single master, or even a single school, Stella explored the great variety of
styles and techniques represented in the museum's collections. According to
Stella's autobiographical notes, he had become enthusiastic about the art of
the Italian Renaissance when he was still in Italy, especially the work of
Giotto, Masaccio, and Mantegna. During his visits to the Metropolitan, he
also became interested in the artists of northern Europe—Van Eyck, Ver-
meer, Rembrandt, Rubens, Holbein, Dürer, and Cranach.[9] By studying the
riches available to him, the young artist acquired skills from the Old Masters
that would allow him the maximum freedom of expression throughout his
career.

Stella left no written record of the works he studied, but his early
drawings suggest that the drawings of the Old Masters were as important for
him as their paintings. With little formal training in draftsmanship, Stella
mastered such various techniques as pen and ink, pencil, chalk, metalpoint,
charcoal, pastel, and red chalk. Stella's versatility and skill as a draftsman are
evident early in his career in such diverse renderings of a single subject as his
numerous drawings of old men (figs. 3–6).

The care and dignity with which he portrayed old people, especially old
men, suggest an attitude of respect and empathy akin to his admiration for
the tradition of Old Master drawings. Wisdom and timelessness were qualities Stella seemed to associate with age and tradition, whether in people or in

Figure 4

Portrait of Bearded Man,
ca. 1909
Silverpoint on prepared
paper
11 ⅝ x 8⅜ in.
Amon Carter Museum,
Fort Worth

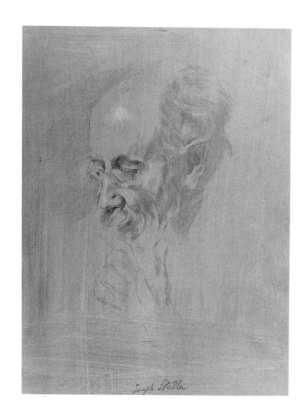

Figure 5

Old Man
Pencil and pastel
16½ x 11½ in.
Jordan-Volpe Gallery,
Inc., New York

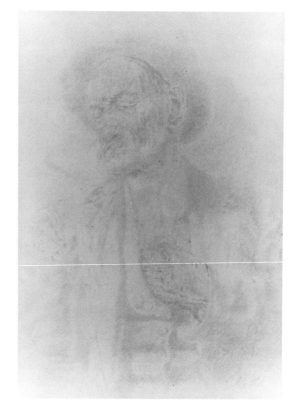

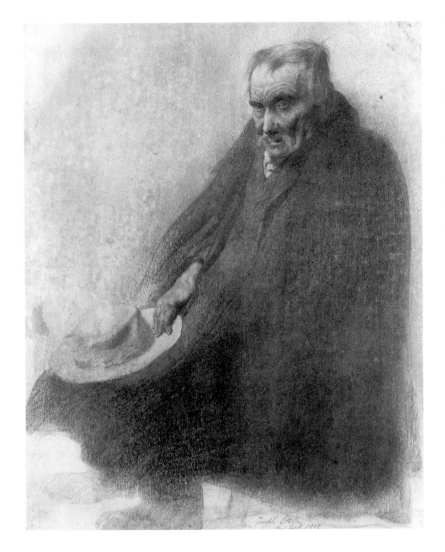

Figure 6

Portrait of an Old Man,
1908
Pencil
11¾ x 9½ in.
Sheldon Memorial Art
Gallery, University of
Nebraska-Lincoln,
Howard S. Wilson
Memorial Collection

art. The old man depicted in *Peasant from Muro Lucano*, executed toward the end of his career, several years after his last trip to Italy, reveals a persistent nostalgia for the land of his birth and the traditional values it represented (fig. 7). The monumentality of the composition and calm dignity of the old peasant, lost in contemplation, contrast with his own late self-portrait (fig. 8). The indistinct, chaotic forms of the background threaten to overwhelm his strong profile, placed lower on the sheet than earlier self-portraits or portraits of other old men. Despite his alert eye and prominent ear, his bald head, sagging chin, furrowed brow, and stooped body suggest the anxieties, physical deterioration, and thoughts of mortality that characterized Stella's last years.

As a young artist at the beginning of his career, Joseph Stella saw America as the country of the future, while Italy represented the grand and noble tradition of the past. Committed to the future and the possibilities it represented, he nonetheless revered traditions and values that had stood the test of time. Throughout his career Stella sought renewal in the work of the Old Master tradition, much as he renewed contact with his own roots through repeated visits to Italy:

> Italy is my only true inspiration. The artist is like a tree: growing older, bent under the weight of its fruit, it presses always closer to the maternal womb that gave it birth. Despite everything, thirty years and more of America have succeeded only in making more solid and firm the latin structure of my nature.[10]

Unlike other young American artists who sought to learn about the most advanced ideas in art by going to study in Paris in the early years of the twentieth century, Stella returned to Italy in 1909 "to renew and rebuild the base and structure" of his art.[11] He visited museums in Florence, Rome, Venice, and Naples to pursue his study of Old Master drawing and painting techniques.

During this trip to Italy, he took up the Renaissance technique of glazing in order to achieve a warmth, depth of color, and transparency that were not possible with a more direct application of paint. He soon realized, however, that there were problems with this approach: "I began to ignore nature and truth, and . . . understood that glazing, although bewitching, and giving me some very fine results, was depriving me of that liberty of movement that a true artist must have."[12] Recognizing that this slow, indirect technique stood in the way of his spontaneous expression, he concluded that "the true lesson given by the old masters is an ethical one, how to organize the personal capacities in order to be true to his own self, how to derive his credit by his own experience lived at his own time, if not to project his vision into the future instead of walking back to the past."[13]

Echoes of Mantegna, Leonardo, Dürer, Rembrandt, Caravaggio, Velázquez, and others reverberate throughout his works on paper, but unlike the lifeless quality of copies, Stella's drawings maintain a freshness and immediacy characteristic of a sensitive drawing from life (figs. 9, 10). His masterful manipulation of colored chalks in *The Bagpipers* invites comparison with eighteenth-century Italian or French artists, but the sensation of breath about to be expelled by the convex cheeks of the two central boys enlivens the faces and conveys an immediacy of experience that transcends any academic exercise (fig. 11). It was not enough for Stella to master the drawing techniques of the Old Masters; he sought to experiment with them as well. In *Woman Resting* (fig. 12) and several other pastels, he manipulated the texture of the pastel surface by rubbing a fine sandpaper over selected areas of the drawing to enhance the rich, tactile quality of the medium.

It may have been Stella's emulation of the Old Masters that inspired him to try his hand at printmaking. His experience with printmaking seems to have been limited to a small number of monotypes (fig. 13) and a group of five etchings (fig. 14).[14] The direct, painterly quality of the monotype seems to have held greater appeal for Stella, since he returned to the medium on several occasions throughout his career. One can only speculate as to why he made no more etchings. If Stella found glazing to be time-consuming and indirect, then he probably abandoned etching for the same reasons. Drawing,

Figure 7

Peasant from Muro Lucano, 1943
Pencil
29¾ x 21¾ in.
Glenn C. Janss Collection

Figure 8

Self-Portrait, early 1940s
Watercolor and charcoal
23¾ x 18⅝ in.
Amon Carter Museum, Fort Worth

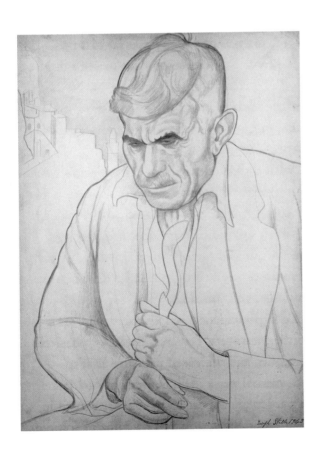

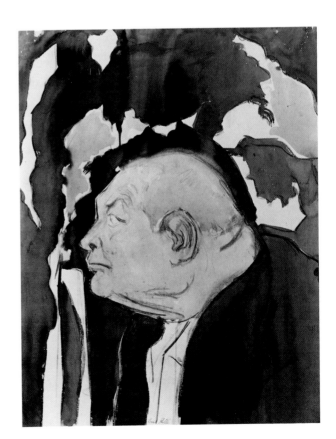

Figure 9

Untitled (Male profiles)
Pencil
9¼ x 7¼ in.
Bernard and Dorothy
Rabin

Figure 10

Pat the Bowery Lord,
ca. 1896–98
Pencil
5⅞ x 3⅞ in.
Robert Schoelkopf
Gallery Ltd., New York

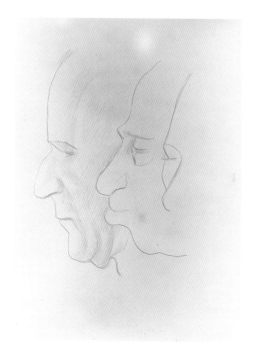

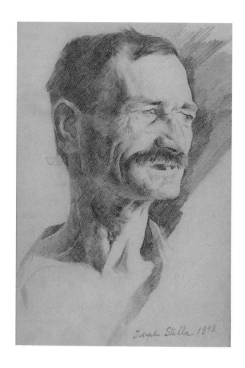

by comparison, was straightforward, unencumbered by special materials or equipment, and allowed for a broad range of line, color, and tone through a variety of portable materials.

Stella continued to seek inspiration in the work of the masters throughout his career. An informal line drawing of a woman's head and shoulders (fig. 15) recalls the shape of Masaccio's monumental figures, and the elegant, linear rendering of a seated nude with a stylized hairdo recalls Ingres's bathers (fig. 16). One of the few drawings directly related to a specific source is his portrait of Helen Walser, a large, color, profile portrait based on Piero della Francesca's *Duchess of Urbino*, of which he owned a photograph (fig. 17).[15]

A series of metalpoint profile portraits of Stella's friends, from the early 1920s, recalls classical relief portraiture as revived by the early Renaissance artist Pisanello in his medals, drawings, and paintings (figs. 18, 19). Carefully modeling the facial contours with delicate hatched and crosshatched lines to create tone and shadow that describe the sitters' features, Stella emphasized the profile outline with repeated strokes and increased pressure as if to immobilize the image into a fixed, eternal mask. His renderings of Marcel Duchamp and Edgard Varèse, in particular, appear to have been carved in stone, while the less severe outlines and delicate touches of color in some of

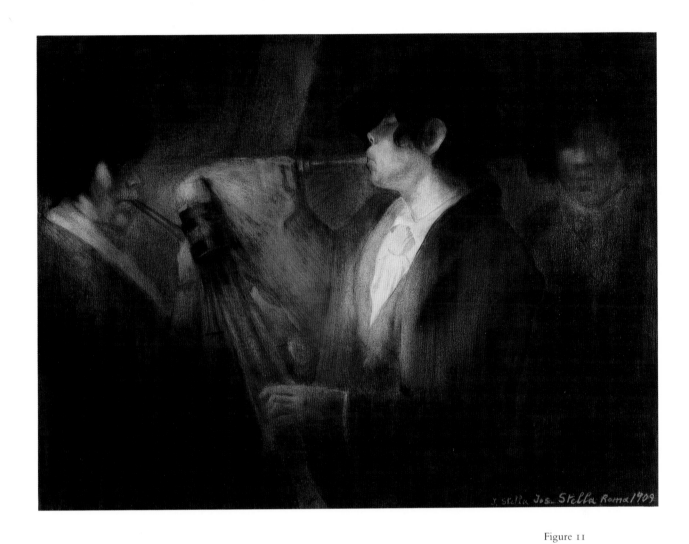

Figure 11

The Bagpipers, 1909
Charcoal, pastel, and
varnish
27 x 36 in.
Richard York Gallery,
New York

Figure 12

Woman Resting
Pencil and crayon
9½ x 7⅜ in.
Private collection

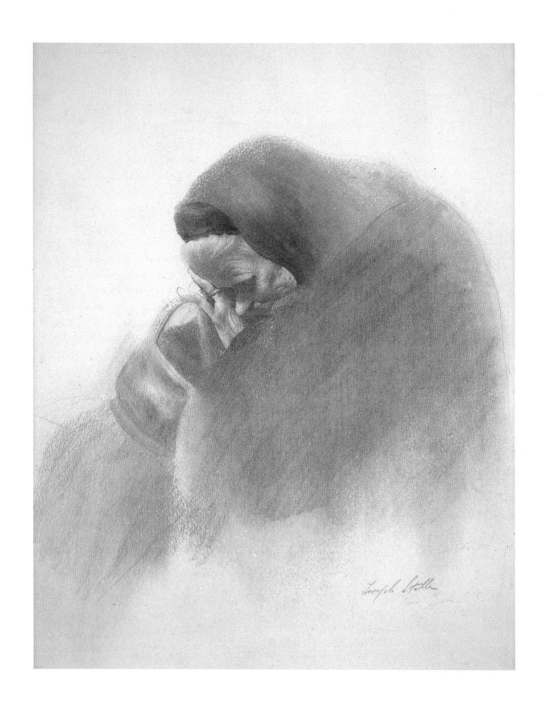

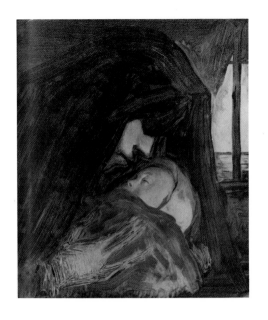

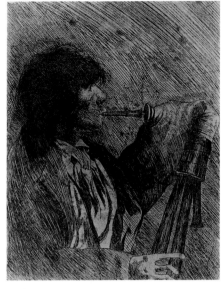

Figure 13

Immigrant Madonna
Monotype
published in *The Survey*,
49 (1 December 1922);
cover
Whereabouts unknown

Figure 14

Untitled (Boy with
bagpipe), ca. 1910
Etching
6¹¹⁄₁₆ x 5⁵⁄₁₆ in.
National Museum of
American Art,
Smithsonian Institution,
Washington, D.C.,
Gift of Bernard Rabin in
memory of Henry A.
Rabin

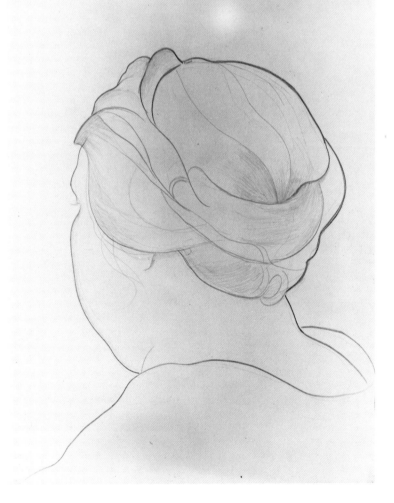

Figure 15

Untitled (Back of
woman's head)
Pencil
14⅛ x 11 in.
Bernard and Dorothy
Rabin

Figure 16

*Back of a Seated Nude
with Blue Ribbon*,
ca. 1924–26
Pencil and crayon on
prepared paper
27½ x 19 in.
Berry-Hill Galleries,
New York

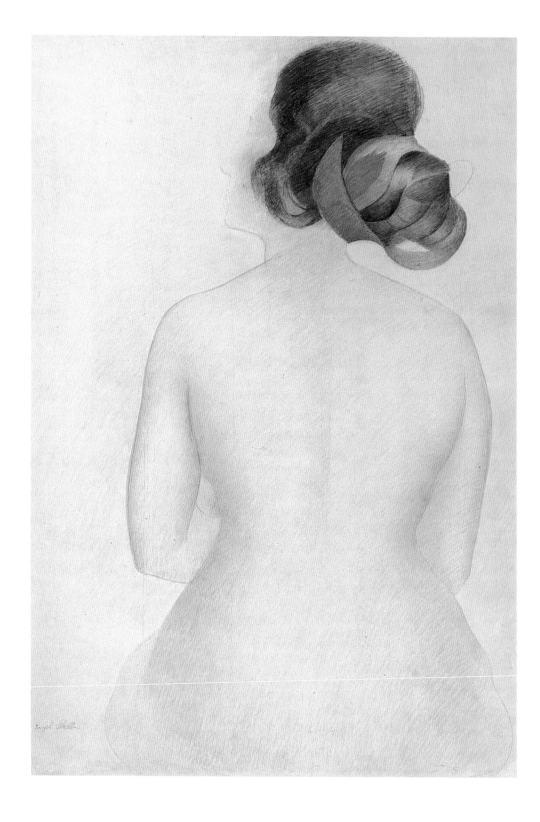

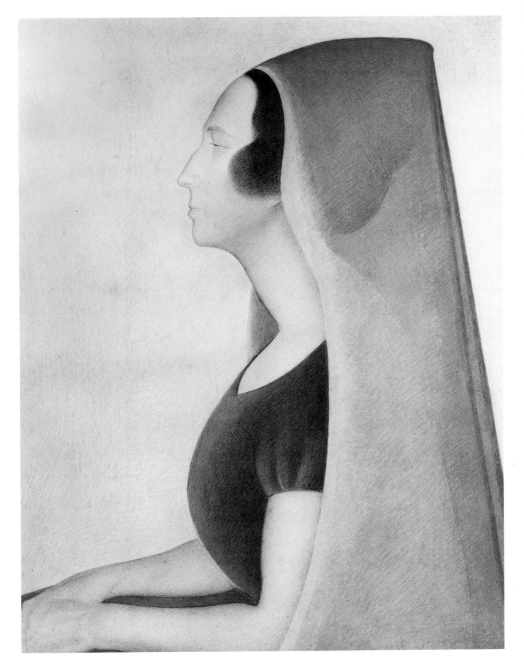

Figure 17

Mrs. Stella (Portrait of the Artist's Wife), ca. 1924–26
Crayon
27 x 21 in.
Yale University Art Gallery, New Haven, Connecticut, Gift of Stephen Carlton Clark

15

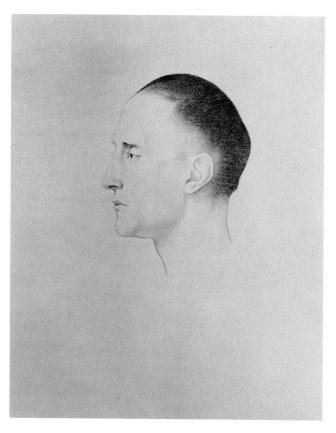

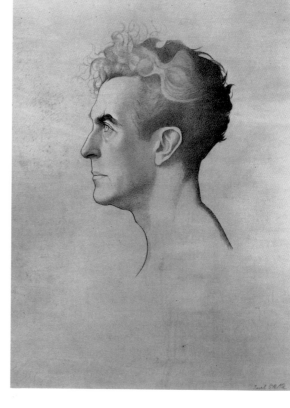

Figure 18

*Portrait of Marcel
Duchamp*, ca. 1920–22
Silverpoint on prepared
paper
27¼ x 21 in.
Collection, The Museum
of Modern Art, New
York, Bequest of
Katherine S. Dreier

Figure 19

Edgard Varèse, ca. 1921
Silverpoint on prepared
paper
20³⁄₁₆ x 14⅝ in.
The Baltimore Museum
of Art, Purchase Fund
(BMA 1963.114)

the other profile portraits suggest a potential for movement rather than iconic permanence. Most of his self-portraits were posed in profile as well, but unlike the clean, white backgrounds in the portraits of his friends, Stella often placed his own image in a context, whether abstract or natural, that suggested a state of mind.

Stella preferred profiles for most of his portrait drawings because he considered this pose more difficult, requiring greater drawing skill and discipline than other poses. Similarly, he relished the challenges of the metalpoint technique:

> For drawing I found the unbending inexorable silverpoint the efficacious tool to seize . . . out of reality integral caustic evidences of life.[16]

> In order to avoid careless facility, I dig my roots obstinately, stubbornly in the crude untaught line buried in the living flesh of the primitives, a line whose purity pours out and flows so surely in the transparency of its sunny clarity. . . . I dedicate my ardent wish to draw with all the precision possible, using the inflexible media of silverpoint and goldpoint that reveal instantly the clearest graphic eloquence.[17]

It is unclear whether Stella read *Il libro dell'arte* (1437) by Cennino Cennini before he returned to Italy in 1909, but Cennino's treatise was Stella's primary source of technical information for the metalpoint drawings as well as for his study of glazing. Emphasizing the importance of drawing, Cennino instructed his reader how to prepare a ground for a metalpoint drawing and pointed out the advantages and characteristics of the three most common metals that were used as a stylus: silver, gold, and lead. Stella seems to have experimented with all three, although it is often difficult to distinguish them with the naked eye.

A deliberate, painstaking technique, metalpoint drawing requires the preparation of an opaque, liquid solution that, when spread on the surface of paper, dries to form a ground with a slight texture or "tooth" that holds minute particles of metal deposited on it when a stylus is dragged along the surface. (Paper treated in this manner is usually called prepared paper.) Traditional formulae for metalpoint ground included such exotic materials as ground chicken bones and rabbit-skin glue, but Stella used a ground of zinc white gouache thinned to the consistency of light cream.[18] If one application of the ground was too thin, he sometimes added a second coat.

Unlike drawing with graphite on paper, the pressure of the metalpoint

Figure 20

Joe Gould, ca. 1919
Pencil and crayon
15 x 12½ in.
Collection, The Museum
of Modern Art,
New York,
The Joan and Lester
Avnet Collection

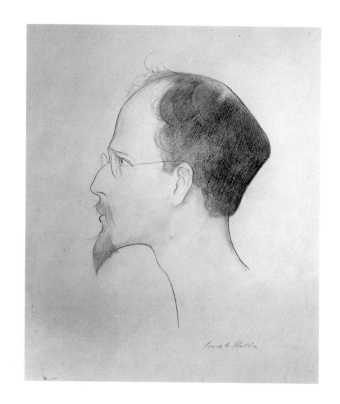

Figure 21

Portrait of Eilshemius,
ca. 1920–22
Silverpoint, crayon, and
pencil with chinese white
on prepared paper
22⅞ x 18¹¹⁄₁₆ in.
Hirshhorn Museum and
Sculpture Garden,
Smithsonian Institution,
Washington, D.C.,
Gift of Joseph H.
Hirshhorn, 1966

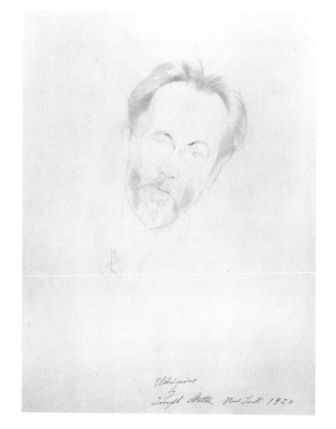

stylus creates a slight incision in the prepared ground that cannot be erased or covered up, requiring certainty and precision by the artist. While the quality of a pencil line can be varied by exerting more or less pressure on the stylus, the quality of a metalpoint line remains uniform and delicate.[19] Too much pressure on the stylus can cause the metalpoint to penetrate the ground and abrade the surface of the paper beneath.

Relishing the challenge to his skills that metalpoint drawing represented, Stella chose this medium to depict the people who represented some of his most intellectually stimulating friends and acquaintances in the early 1920s. Marcel Duchamp and composer Edgard Varèse were leaders among the avant-garde, while Joe Gould and Louis Eilshemius were eccentric bohemians (figs. 20, 21).[20] Rendering their likenesses in lines of precious metal, Stella idealized and immortalized his subjects by alluding to the eternal values symbolized by silver and gold. To depict such avant-garde, bohemian types in classical profile using such a refined, traditional medium as metalpoint drawing was to suggest that the enfants terribles of today will be revered as tomorrow's Old Masters.

"Not one day without a line"

The hundreds of informal sketches of people, a visual diary of images, of which only a few eventually found their way into his paintings, suggest that for Stella drawing served as a means of observing and recording the world around him. The varied papers he used, often of poor quality and uneven size, indicate that drawing was often informal, an immediate means of recording his thoughts, impressions, or observations at any time, in any situation.

Stella looked upon his sketches not merely as a dictionary of images from which to select at a later date, but as a source of creative inspiration. In his personal notes he disclosed how integral his drawings were for his artistic vision: "Some [visions] reveal themselves in fragments to reappear in their fullness, to be pursued and seized little by little by a patient, obdurate daily practice: *Nulla dies sine linea* [not one day without a line]," a quotation he often repeated and attributed to Giotto.[21]

Although one is tempted to view a drawing related to a painting as a study for the painting, this relationship implicitly denies the independent achievement of the work on paper. Stella's portrait of Helen Walser (see fig. 17) was completed around 1926, and the painting based on it was not done until 1940.[22] In other instances, when a related drawing and painting were completed at approximately the same time, as were Stella's silverpoint portrait of Kathleen Millay (fig. 22) and the painting entitled *Amazon* (fig. 23), the drawing is quite different in character and expression from the painting.[23] He transformed the delicate, classical image of the drawing into a bold, aggressive, abstracted form that looms over a distant landscape. Was his forceful, frontal depiction of his friend an intermediate step in the transformation of his subject from a portrait to a symbol (fig. 24)? In this crayon and colored pencil portrait of Millay, he transformed the classical profile into a dramatic image of a modern woman who engages the viewer with a direct,

Figure 22

Portrait of Kathleen Millay, ca. 1924
Silverpoint and crayon on prepared paper
27⅜ x 22⅜ in.
The Lowe Art Museum, The University of Miami, Bequest of Ann Eckert Keenan

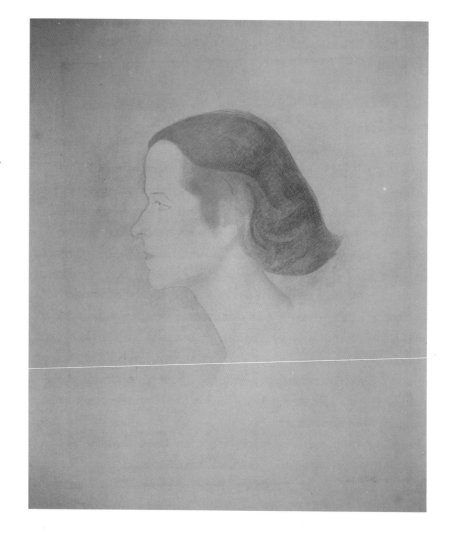

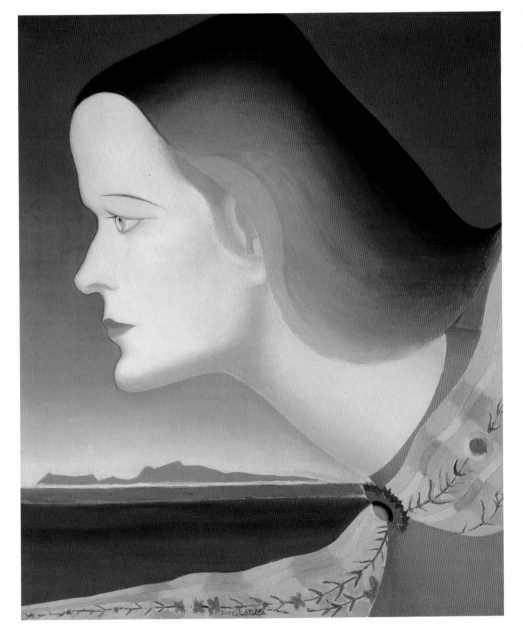

Figure 23

Amazon, 1924
Oil on canvas
27 x 22 in.
Richard York Gallery,
New York

Figure 24

(opposite)

Kathleen Millay, ca. 1924
Silverpoint, red crayon,
and colored pencil on
prepared paper
28 x 22 in.
The Fine Arts Center,
Cheekwood, Nashville

confrontational stare that heightens the sensuality of the bare flesh, curvilinear rhythms, and intense red-orange background. The unique character of the three portraits suggests that Stella conceived of each of them as an independent work of art despite their strong similarities.

Similarly, the metamorphosis from drawing to painting in such works as *Biskra* or *Song of Birds* highlights the distinctive qualities of the drawing (figs. 25, 26). The flat, geometric composition of *Biskra*, crowned by an exuberant array of palm fronds that fill the upper half of the sheet, presents a timeless, emblematic image of North Africa in which a delicate balance between human presence and nature has been achieved. Unlike the harder forms of the painted version, the soft individual pencil strokes create a sense of a diffuse, white light that bathes the forms and minimizes shadows. In the drawing of sparrows on a cherry branch, the graceful simplicity of the composition, delicate modeling of the feathers, symbolic associations of a trinity, and subtle variations in pose are subsumed by the complex play of color and form in the painting *Song of the Birds*, which has its own appeal as a decorative ensemble (fig. 27). Stella's sensitive exploration of the possibilities and limitations of each medium in which he worked distinguishes his drawings from the more mundane creations of less skillful draftsmen.

A number of drawings have been associated with Stella's monumental paintings *Brooklyn Bridge* and *The Voice of the City of New York Interpreted* (figs. 28, 29), but it is not always clear whether the drawings were actually studies for the painting or were simply sketches of the same subject done either before or after the painting was completed.[24] Such a work as *Study for "New York Interpreted: Brooklyn Bridge"* captures the looming mystery and spiritual intensity of the earlier painting as well as the iconic symmetry and monumentality of the later one, suggesting that it may have been executed between the two paintings, but Stella's method of working often confounds such logical assumptions (fig. 30). The mazelike profusion of cables in another study of the Brooklyn Bridge does not necessarily mean that this pastel drawing preceded the 1919 painting, which is based on a similar compositional device (fig. 31). In contrast to his painted versions of the Brooklyn Bridge, these two drawings are energized by a spontaneity of expression and intensity of feeling that are masked by the formality of the finished paintings.

Similarly, Stella's drawings of New York skyscrapers often transform the physical appearance of these buildings into lyrical abstractions (figs. 32, 33). The simple geometric forms, water-softened edges, and transparent washes create a sense of light and air-filled space quite unlike his verbal

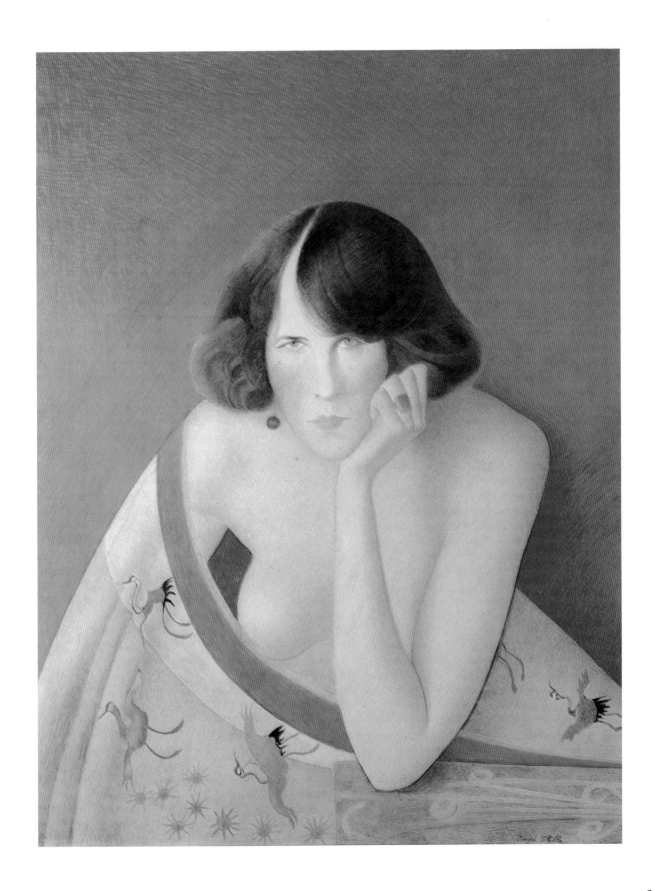

Figure 25

Biskra, 1930
Crayon and pencil
14⅛ x 10⅛ in.
Barbara Mathes Gallery,
New York

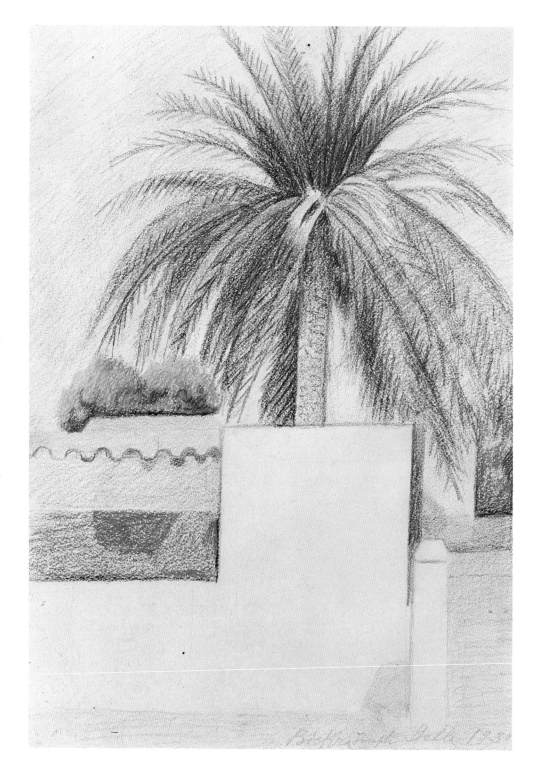

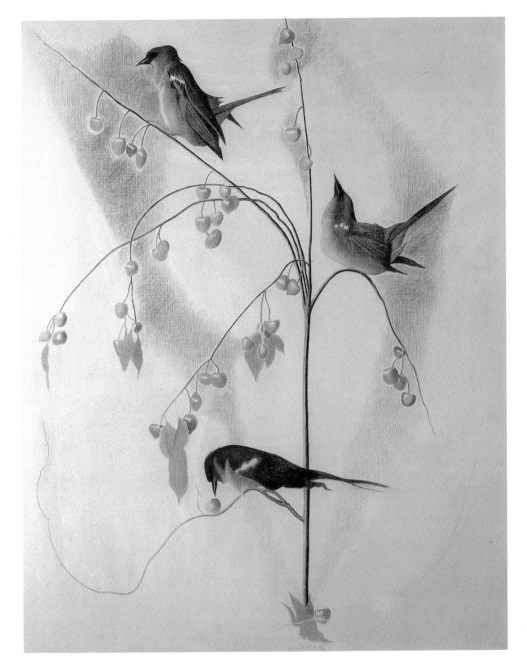

Figure 26

Song of Birds, ca. 1920–26
Silverpoint and colored
pencil on prepared paper
26¾ x 20¾ in.
Harvey and Françoise
Rambach

Figure 27

Song of the Birds, 1920–26
Oil on canvas
42¼ x 32¼ in.
William C. Janss
Collection

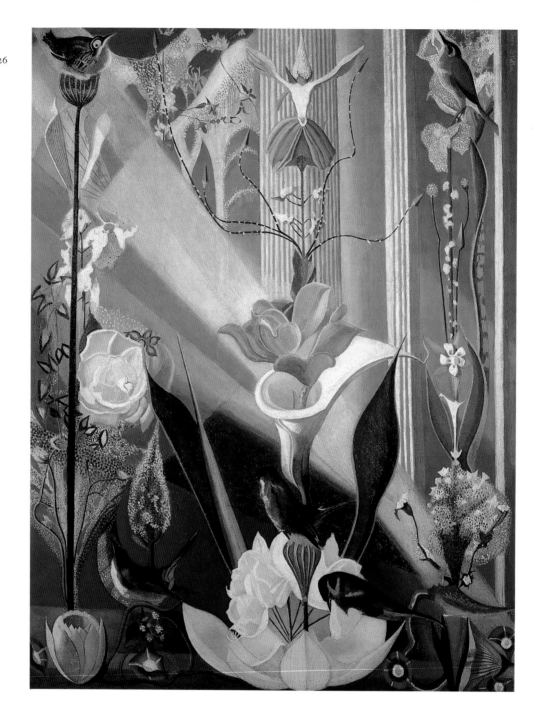

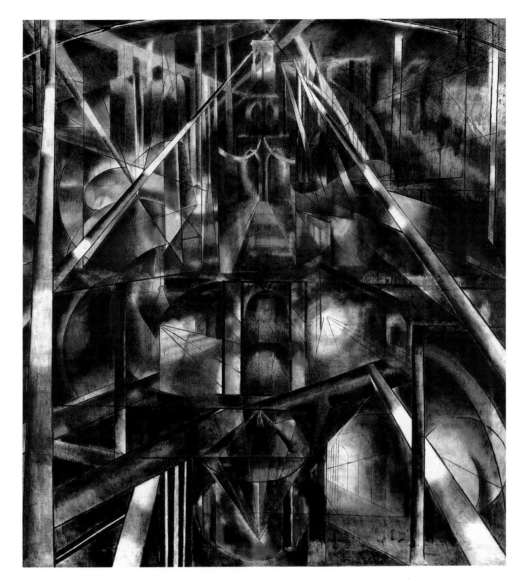

Figure 28

Brooklyn Bridge, ca. 1919
Oil on canvas
84 x 76 in.
Yale University Art
Gallery, New Haven,
Connecticut, Collection
Société Anonyme

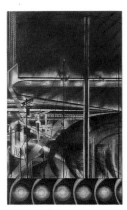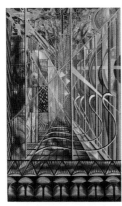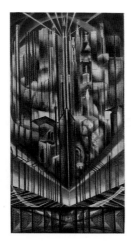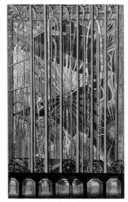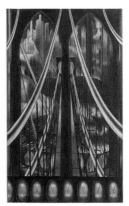

Figure 29

The Voice of the City of New York Interpreted, 1920–22
Oil and tempera on canvas
99¾ x 270 in. (5 panels)
Newark Museum, New Jersey, Purchase 1937, Felix Fuld Bequest Fund

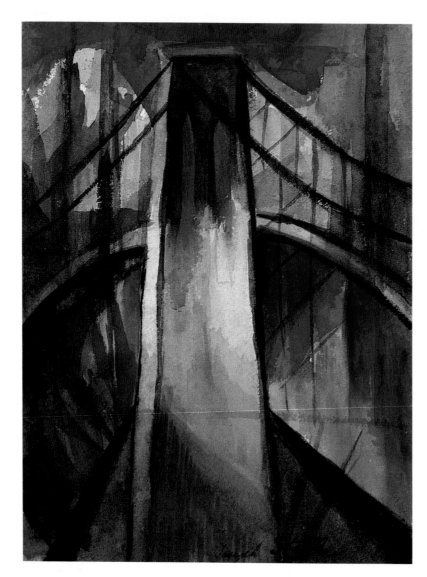

Figure 30

Study for "New York Interpreted: Brooklyn Bridge," ca. 1919–21
Watercolor and brush and ink
13¹⁵⁄₁₆ x 9¹⁵⁄₁₆ in.
Hirshhorn Museum and Sculpture Garden, Smithsonian Institution, Washington, D.C., Gift of Joseph H. Hirshhorn, 1966

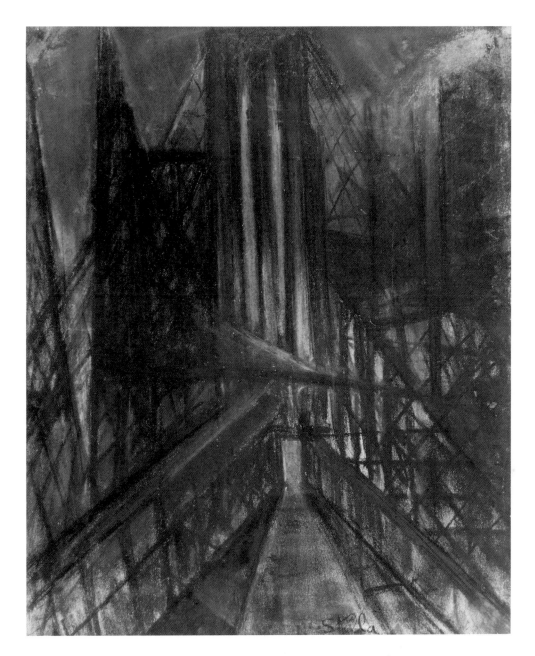

Figure 31

Sketch for "Brooklyn Bridge"
Pastel
21 x 17½ in.
Collection of Whitney
Museum of American
Art, New York,
Gift of Miss Rose Fried
(52.36)

Figure 32

Building Forms,
ca. 1915–20
Watercolor and pencil on
paper mounted on
paperboard
24¾ x 18¼ in.
Hirshhorn Museum and
Sculpture Garden,
Smithsonian Institution,
Washington, D.C.,
Gift of Joseph H.
Hirshhorn, 1966

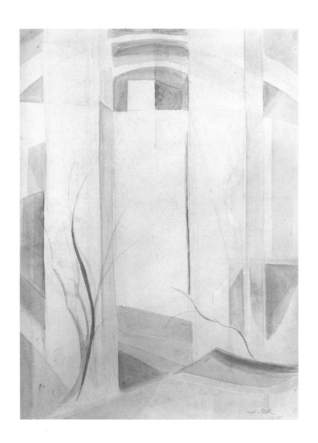

Figure 33

Skyscrapers, ca. 1920
Watercolor and pencil
23⅛ x 16⅝ in.
Albright-Knox Art
Gallery, Buffalo
Charles Clifton and
Edmund Hayes Funds,
1975

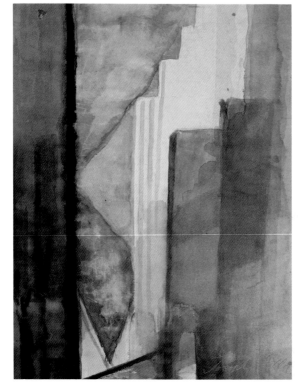

description of "skyscrapers like bandages covering the sky, stifling our breath."[25] In other compositions of skyscrapers, the sense of looming claustrophobia is more pronounced (fig. 34). Still others are characterized by bright, contrasting colors and lively rhythms that convey the energy of New York's vitality and excitement (figs. 35, 36). If his impressive polyptych *The Voice of the City of New York Interpreted* embodies Stella's epic version of this subject, his works on paper represent his poetic visions of the city in their more intuitive form. In contrast to the more careful planning of the painting, the forms, colors, and rhythms of the drawings capture the rawness and immediacy of his emotional reactions without the refinements of conscious organization that transform the elements into decorative patterns and a harmonious whole.

"Life flowing unaware"

Even before Stella recognized the inhibiting aspects of relying too strongly on the study of the Old Masters during his first trip to Italy in 1909–10, he had devoted much of his time to drawing the world around him, especially the people he encountered in his immediate surroundings. After his relatively brief experience in art school, Stella avoided working from professional models in favor of more spontaneous sketches of people engaged in their daily activities:

> Soon I became very busy in drawing from the most striking characters that I could hunt in the streets, in the parks and in the lodging houses of the slums. My chief concern . . . was to catch life flowing unaware with its spontaneous eloquent aspects, not stiffened or deadened by the pose.[26]

Carlo de Fornaro recalled that "this irresistable [*sic*] itch to draw humanity all around him almost got him into trouble with the loafers, bums and drunkards, who were sitting or sprawling on the benches or upon the grass in the parks, and they resented it almost to the point of violence. . . . Thus our eager artist was forced to sketch surreptitiously by placing his pad upon a newspaper so that his camouflage lulled his victims into natural poses."[27]

Stella's preference for drawing real people instead of studio models persisted throughout his career. The large number of sketches of the backs of people's heads suggests that he often drew people sitting in front of him on a

Figure 34

City Buildings, New York,
1917
Watercolor
$11^{11}/_{16}$ x $9^{1}/_{4}$ in.
The Ackland Art
Museum, The University
of North Carolina at
Chapel Hill, Gift of Mr.
and Mrs. J. Lanier
Williams in memory of
J. Lanier Williams, Jr.

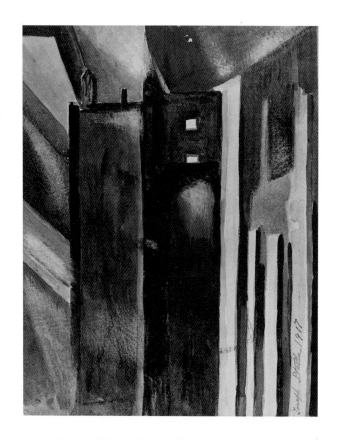

Figure 35

New York, ca. 1920–26
Watercolor and gouache
on textured paper
$29^{1}/_{2}$ x $23^{1}/_{2}$ in.
Mr. and Mrs. Vincent A.
Carrozza

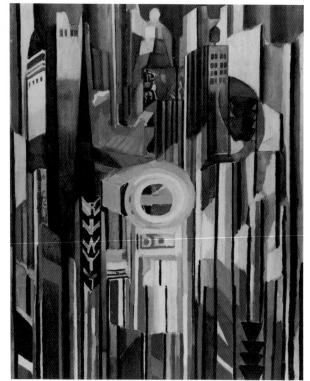

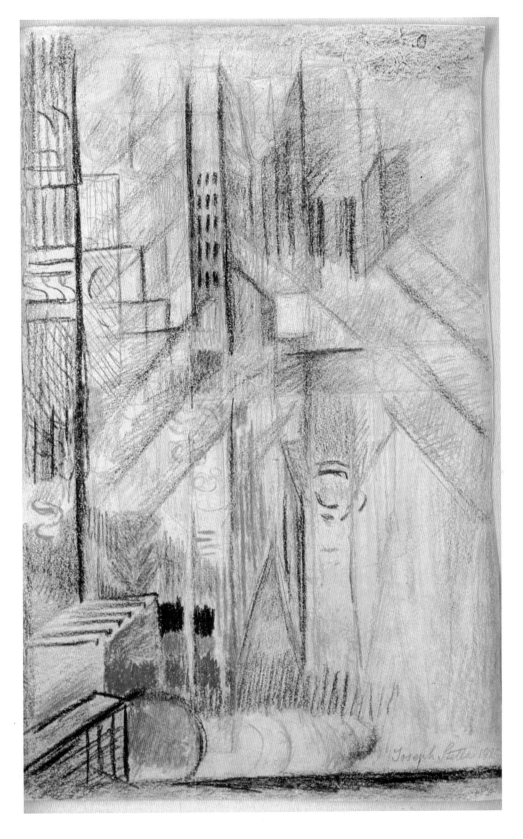

Figure 36

Study for "New York Interpreted," 1925
Crayon and pencil
12½ x 8 in.
Mr. and Mrs. Paul Sack

33

bus or subway, oblivious to his scrutiny (fig. 37). Another singular pose that Stella favored was that of sleeping figures, whose stillness allowed him to draw from life over an extended period of time without hiring models (figs. 38–41). The intimacy of watching a fellow creature asleep brought out the tender, emotional side of Stella's personality that he rarely revealed in his paintings. He captured the poignancy of Denise Walser and his dog Fat Darling asleep in each other's arms through his simple linear rendering and the close-up vantage point from which he observed the sleeping girl and his beloved dog.

Moreover, the semiconscious state of sleep seems to have represented for Stella the free association of thoughts and images, unimpeded by reason or logic, that fostered imagination and creativity. Unlike the more formal, complex compositions of his paintings, Stella's drawings reveal the personal, intuitive side of his creative process. As he drew the sleeping cat, the form suggested a fetal position that Stella reinforced by strengthening the outline of the animal to transform it into an embryonic shape. The act of drawing itself seems to have inspired his imagination in a way that thought or observation alone could not.

To satisfy his predilection for "curious types, revealing, with the unrestrained eloquence of their masks the crude story of their life,"[28] Stella had to go no further than the teeming streets of his own neighborhood on the Lower East Side of New York, the Bowery, or nearby Ellis Island to find people of various nationalities, ages, and circumstances. An immigrant himself, he was fascinated with the human melting pot around him. Immigrants of diverse nationalities either posed for Stella or were sketched unawares by the artist who captured concisely and perceptively the salient features of their physiognomies, dress, and temperament, with no hint of caricature or exaggeration (figs. 42, 43). The monumental pose in which he chose to depict them often emphasized their quiet dignity.

Stella's stylistic and emotional ties to the Old Master tradition were intimately involved in his own sentiments as an immigrant and the dual loyalties he felt toward the new world and the old. Despite the advantages of a comfortable, middle-class life, the Stella family left their homeland for the "land of opportunity," just as had masses of uneducated Italian immigrants who landed on the shores of the United States in the late nineteenth century. Unlike most other immigrants, whose entire energies were absorbed by the need to find jobs and provide for families, Joseph Stella had the opportunity to continue his studies in New York and eventually to pursue his interest in

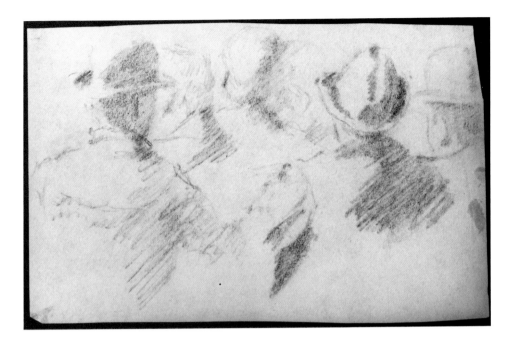

Figure 37

Untitled (Heads of seated men)
Pencil
7¾ x 5 in.
Bernard and Dorothy
Rabin

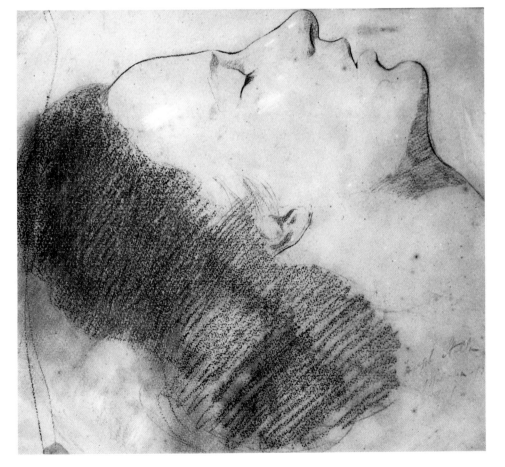

Figure 38

*Profile Head of a Sleeping
Woman*, ca. 1909
Charcoal, crayon, and
colored chalk
9⅜ x 10¾ in.
Allen Memorial Art
Museum, Oberlin, Ohio,
Charles F. Olney Fund
(77.17)

35

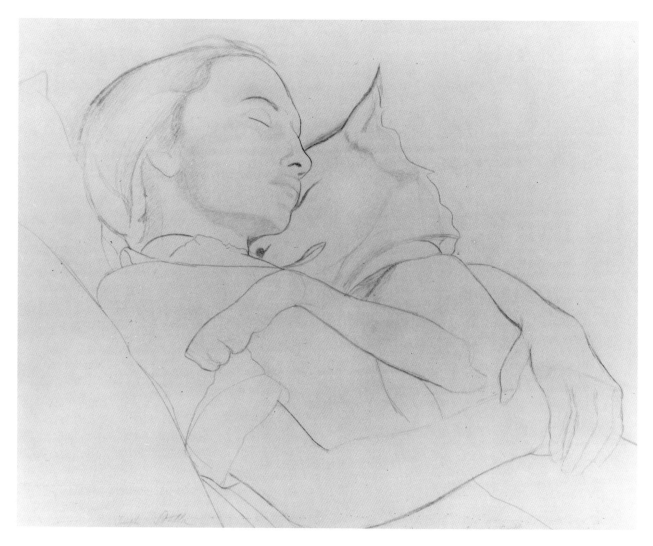

Figure 39

Denise Walser and Stella's
Dog, ca. 1921–26
Silverpoint on prepared
paper
17 x 22½ in.
Private collection

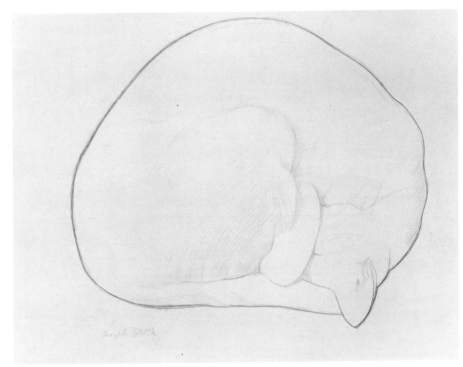

Figure 40

Sleeping Cat
Pencil
10¾ x 13¼ in.
Jordan-Volpe Gallery,
Inc., New York

Figure 41

Portrait of Clara Fasano,
1944
Pencil and pastel
12 x 18 in.
National Museum of
American Art,
Smithsonian Institution,
Washington, D.C.

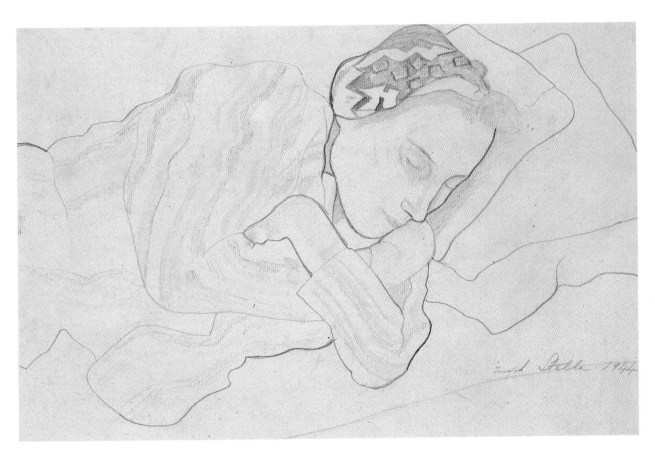

Figure 42

Immigrant Girl—Ellis Island, 1916
Charcoal
29 x 14⅛ in.
Hirshhorn Museum and
Sculpture Garden,
Smithsonian Institution,
Washington, D.C.,
The Joseph H. Hirshhorn
Bequest

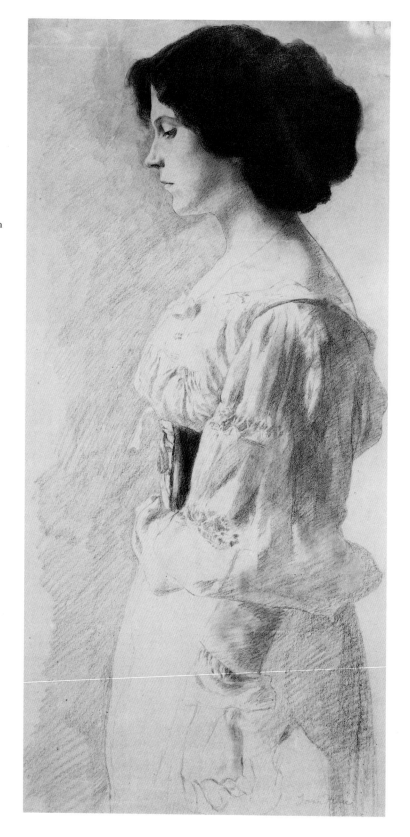

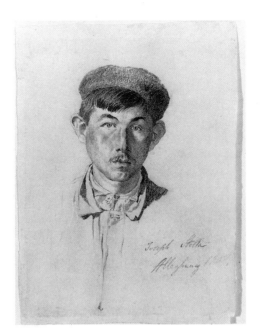

Figure 43

A Greener: Lad from Herzegovina, 1908
Pencil and white gouache
6⅜ x 4¾ in.
The Saint Louis Art Museum,
Purchase: Friends of the Saint Louis Art Museum

art. He did not face the same harsh realities of other immigrants. Stella could return to Italy if he chose. Although his education, middle-class background, and artistic training separated him from the great majority of illiterate, manual laborers who made up the bulk of the immigrant population, Stella shared many of their folk superstitions and was sympathetic to their problems, especially those associated with prejudice against their national origins. Stella took pride in his Italian background and the centuries of culture and tradition that it represented.

In 1905, at the possible prompting of his brother Antonio, who was active in immigrant affairs, some of Stella's drawings were brought to the attention of the Reverend Lyman Abbott and William H. Howland, editor and treasurer respectively of the social reform weekly newspaper *The Outlook.* Seven drawings appeared as illustrations for "Americans in the Rough," an article in the 23 December 1905 issue of the newspaper. From the concise, linear vignette of *Irish Types* to the broader, more intense and dramatic rendering of *A Russian Jew,* Stella's seven drawings—illustrating six different nationalities, each on a page of its own, with a depiction of the gateway to Ellis Island on the title page—enliven the presentation and testify to the great variety of drawing styles in which he worked.[29] The next year Stella provided illustrations for Ernest Poole's novel *The Voice of the Street.* More anecdotal in character, these illustrations relate directly to the text they accompany and were more melodramatic and sentimental than his other drawings.

Either through the publication of these drawings or perhaps again by virtue of Antonio's connections, Stella received numerous commissions between 1907 and 1924 to provide drawings for use as illustrations in *The Survey*, a publication dedicated to social welfare and reform. His first commission for this magazine came in late 1907, when he was asked to visit the site of a devastating mine disaster in Monongah, West Virginia, with Paul Kellogg, a reporter for the magazine who later became its publisher. He provided four illustrations for Kellogg's article on the subject in the 4 January 1908 issue of *The Survey*, and later that year he was asked to contribute illustrations to accompany a sociological study of the workers and working conditions of Pittsburgh, a series of articles that came to be known as "The Pittsburgh Survey."[30]

This commission provided Stella with the opportunity to visit Pittsburgh, an experience that fired his imagination:

> I was greatly impressed by Pittsburgh. It was a real revelation. Often shrouded by fog and smoke, her black mysterious mass—cut in the middle by the fantastic, tortuous Allegheny River, and like a battlefield, ever pulsating, throbbing with the innumerable explosions of its steel mills—was like the stunning realization of some of the most stirring infernal regions sung by Dante. In the thunderous voice of the wind, that at times with the most genial fury was lashing here and there fog and smoke to change the scenario for new, unexpected spectacles, I could hear the bitter pungent Dantesque *terzina*.[31]

Although most of the drawings made for "The Pittsburgh Survey" were of workers (figs. 44–46), the most intriguing illustrations are those of the city of Pittsburgh, the workers' houses (figs. 47, 48), and mill interiors (fig. 49). Unlike the powerful message of social reform conveyed in the articles they accompanied, Stella's drawings reveal a vivid poetic imagination that transforms the grimy, industrial city, the wretched working conditions, and the workers' dingy hovels into dramatic excerpts from the *Divine Comedy*. Carlo de Fornaro recalled Stella's remark that "the American tramp of that period was like a king who had freely abdicated enforced labor for a free life."[32] Stella regarded the figure depicted in *Old Man Sleeping in a Field* as a rebellious spirit who asserted the power of the individual by rejecting economic slavery in a willful challenge to organized, orderly society (fig. 50).

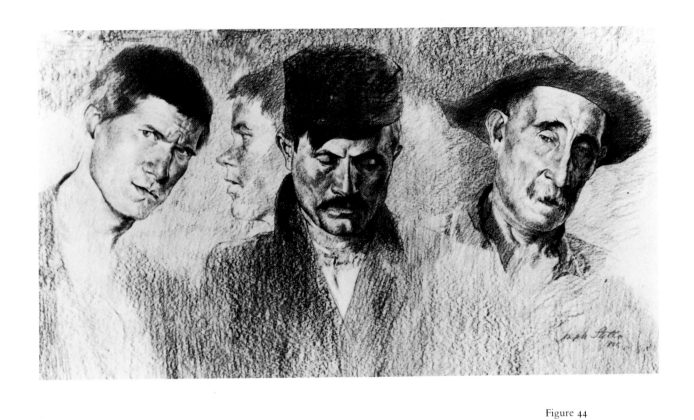

Figure 44

In the Bread Line at Wood's Run (Four Miners), ca. 1908
Charcoal
18¼ x 34⅜ in.
Published in *The Survey*,
21 (6 March 1909)
Whereabouts unknown

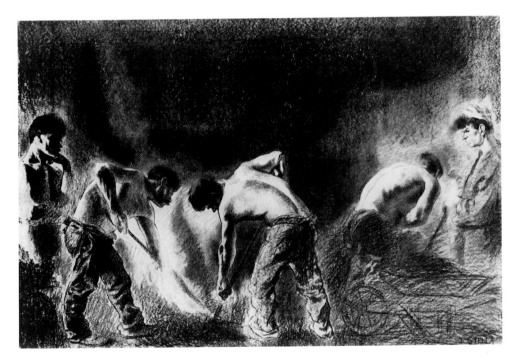

Figure 45

At the Base of the Blast Furnace, ca. 1908
Charcoal and pastel (?)
Published in *The Survey*,
21 (6 March 1909)
Whereabouts unknown

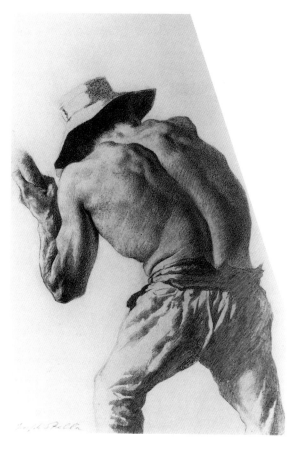

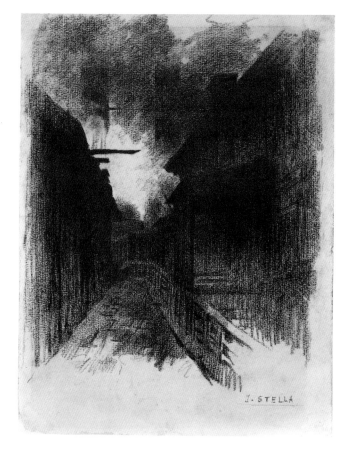

Figure 46

Untitled (Back of a man
working), ca. 1908
Pencil
9¼ x 6⅝ in.
Bernard and Dorothy
Rabin

Figure 47

*Street in Allegheny
(Company Houses)*, 1908
Charcoal
13¾ x 9½ in. (irregular)
Published in *The Survey*,
21 (6 February 1909)
Collection, The Museum
of Modern Art,
New York,
Gift of Mrs. Bliss
Parkinson

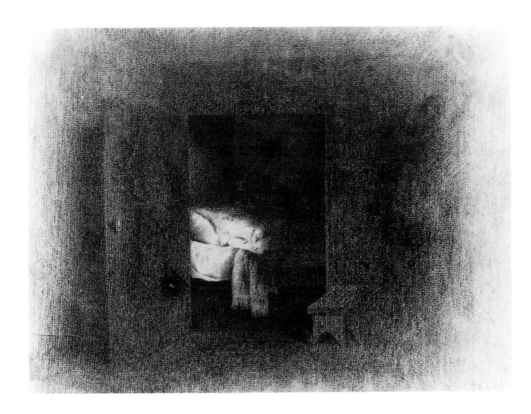

Figure 48

The Hole in the Wall (Painter's Row: Dark Bedroom), ca. 1908
Charcoal
12½ x 16½ in.
Published in *The Survey,* 21 (6 March 1909)
Private collection

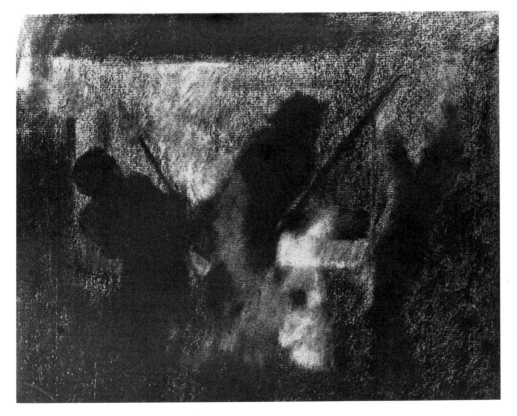

Figure 49

Before the Furnace Door, ca. 1908
Charcoal (?)
Published in *The Survey,* 21 (6 March 1909)
Whereabouts unknown

43

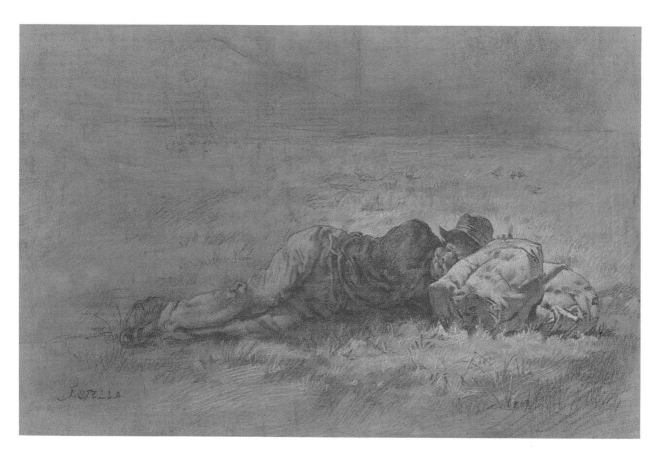

Figure 50

Old Man Sleeping in a Field, ca. 1908
Gouache and chalk
11 x 16¹³⁄₁₆ in.
The Carnegie Museum
of Art, Pittsburgh,
Copperweld, Hafner
Fund and Fine Arts
Discretionary Fund

The warm, protective glow that bathes the subtly rendered gouache and chalk drawing of an old tramp asleep idealizes the figure, who might have been portrayed as a miserable wretch or troublesome social problem.

For Stella, energized by the change of scene and the drama it afforded, the commission itself seems to have become secondary. He created more than one hundred drawings while he was in Pittsburgh: "I worked with fury for *The Survey* and for myself."[33] Some of his most dramatic and evocative drawings were not reproduced in "The Pittsburgh Survey" articles, although they were included in exhibitions of *The Survey* drawings in Pittsburgh, New York, and Chicago (figs. 51, 52).

He continued to submit drawings to be used as illustrations in *The Survey* sporadically through 1924, with some of the Pittsburgh drawings reappearing or appearing for the first time in subsequent issues or in other publications.[34] While an artist's drawings are usually more private and personal than his paintings, many of Stella's early drawings were his most public works and were more widely seen than his paintings. A monumental figure such as *Immigrant Girl—Ellis Island* (see fig. 42) is clearly a major, independent portrait despite the anecdotal legend that accompanied it when it appeared in *The Survey* magazine.[35]

The subjects of Stella's early figure drawings—immigrants, laborers, mothers, children, vagabonds, and characters who peopled the streets of New York's Lower East Side, ordinary people engaged in their everyday activities, and scenes of their urban environment—beg comparison with works of a similar nature by the artists who came to be known as the "Ashcan School" for their realistic depictions of the more mundane aspects of city life. Like many of them, Stella helped support himself with commissions for illustrations while he pursued his career as a painter, but the superficial similarities mask profound differences that link Stella to an entirely different tradition in American art.

Certainly Stella was familiar with the works of John Sloan, George Luks, Jerome Myers, Eugene Higgins, Robert Henri, and others, whose exhibitions in New York at the Alan Gallery, National Arts Club, and Macbeth Gallery elicited attention and controversy. Scorned by their critics as "apostles of ugliness" or "the revolutionary black gang," these artists rebelled against the more genteel traditions of the academies and expressed the vitality of contemporary life in their broad, direct, sketchy drawings and paintings. Although their painting styles owed much to such masters as Hals and Velázquez, their illustrative, journalistic approach was anathema to traditional draftsmen.

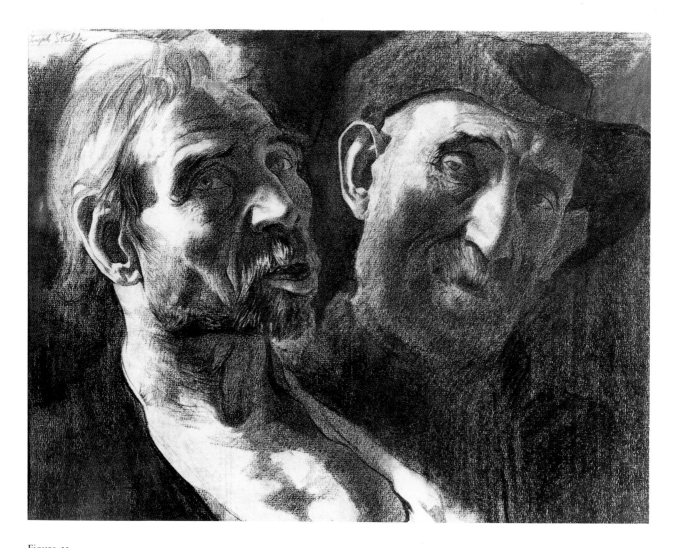

Figure 51

Miners, ca. 1908
Charcoal
37 x 19⅛ in.
Yale University Art
Gallery, New Haven,
Connecticut, John
Heinz III Fund

46

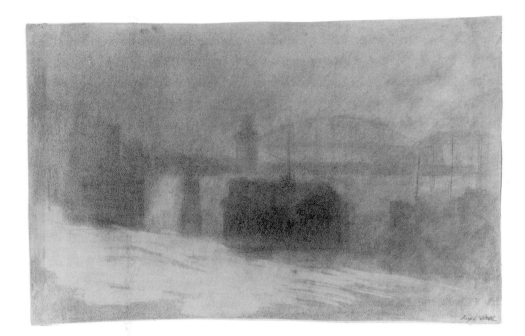

Figure 52

Bridge, ca. 1908
Charcoal
14⁹⁄₁₆ x 23½ in.
The Carnegie Museum
of Art, Pittsburgh,
Howard N. Eavenson
Memorial Fund (58.62)

In 1913 Stella recalled that, before his recent trip to Italy and Paris, his "enthusiasm for the old art . . . was rising higher and higher on account of the vulgarity of the current exhibitions."[36] Despite his enthusiastic involvement with contemporary subjects, such as those in "The Pittsburgh Survey," he continued to rely heavily on the Old Master tradition for his drawing and painting techniques, compositional principles, and sometimes for allegorical content as well. Classically framed by two standing figures at the edges of the composition in *At the Base of the Blast Furnace* (see fig. 45), the studied, reciprocal poses of the two central workers and the friezelike arrangement of the carefully modeled figures recall Mantegna or Pollaiuolo more readily than the more informal compositions and spontaneous renderings of his contemporaries. *In the Bread Line at Wood's Run (Four Miners)* presents an allegory of the three ages of man—youth, maturity, and old age—in modern guise (see fig. 44). The carefully rendered anatomy depicted in *Untitled* (Back of a man working) recalls Michelangelo's solid, sculptural figures more directly than the matter-of-fact, journalistic approach of his contemporaries (see fig. 46).

In other drawings, Stella re-created the baroque drama of "the spasm and pathos of those workers condemned to a very strenuous life, exposed to the constant MENACE OF DEATH."[37] Shadowy, abstracted forms, reminiscent of Saint Sebastian's tormentors thrusting their spears, are startled by the miraculous apparition of a glowing cross, a scene with strong overtones of a religious conversion and a mysterious dance of death, like a vision from Dante's *Inferno* (see fig. 49). Such literary and religious allusions were rejected outright by Henri and his followers, whose "slice-of-life" realism called for a more direct expression.

Tonalist Abstraction

Stella's dramatic divergence from the stark realist approach of the Ashcan artists is equally pronounced in his lyrical and romantic impressions of the city of Pittsburgh. Instead of depicting the people, activities, and locales of urban life, Stella transformed the fog and smoke of the damp climate and industrial pollution into a mysterious haze that softened the harsh outlines and industrial skyline into a picturesque panorama. The church steeple in the foreground of *Chimneys, Pittsburgh* and *Pittsburgh, Winter*, juxtaposed in the center of the composition with the towering smokestacks, anticipates the quasi-religious paean to modern industrial prowess that Stella expressed more than a decade later in his monumental painting of the Brooklyn Bridge (figs. 53, 54).[38] Investing a scene such as *Pittsburgh, Winter* with spiritual, even religious, overtones, Stella expressed hope for redemption in the natural beauty that enveloped the grimy and discordant by-products of industrialization:

> I was in Pittsburgh and winter was raging. It had been snowing day and night, and a sharp wind was blowing, unmercifully lashing the poor mortals. The candor of the snow was intensified, magnified by the black sky eternally black and throbbing with black smoke luridly sincopated [*sic*] here and there by bloody spots. The tragic town of the steel mills seemed transformed. She had lost that oppressive atmosphere of a damned infernal city. But the black imprint on the snow [was] becoming more and more conspicuous. The true dark personality of the town was ever asserting itself, and this ermine dress was like an ironical white dress of the first communion, barely concealing the hard-boiled structure of a civic arpy.[39]

If Stella's noble, monumental workers conveyed a message complementary to the articles they were intended to illustrate, his lyrical, romantic views

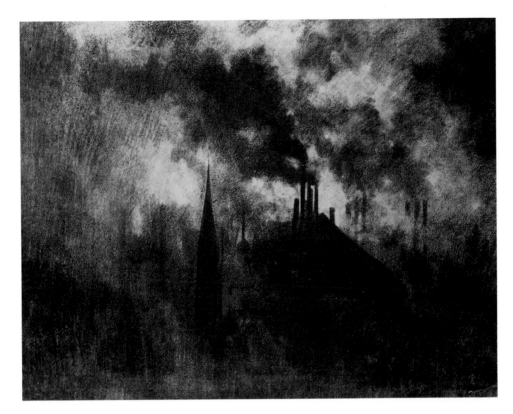

Figure 53

Chimneys, Pittsburgh,
ca. 1908
Charcoal
18¼ x 23⅞ in.
Mr. and Mrs. Meyer P.
Potamkin

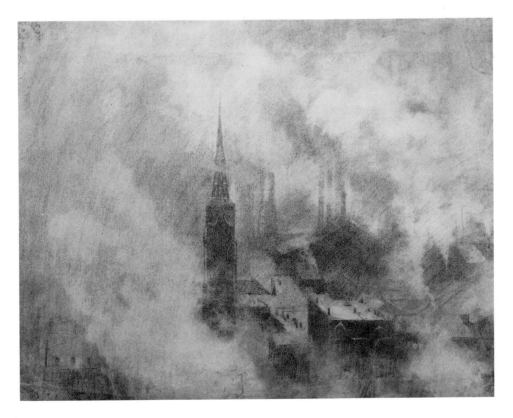

Figure 54

Pittsburgh, Winter,
ca. 1908
Charcoal
17⅛ x 23 in.
Rita and Daniel Fraad

49

of the city were in direct contrast to the stark, journalistic content of "The Pittsburgh Survey." Instead, they are strongly reminiscent of the poetic, tonalist sensibility of James McNeill Whistler, whose paintings, drawings, and prints were well known and widely available in America. Drawings such as *Bridge* (see fig. 52) and *Street in Allegheny* (see fig. 47) are especially reminiscent of Whistler's emphasis on the spiritual, abstract qualities of a composition at the expense of objective description. The intimate, picturesque view of a street where unsanitary, unsafe living conditions were probably the norm recalls such early etchings by Whistler as *Street at Saverne* or, even more closely, such later etchings of Venice as *Nocturne: Palaces* in which the details of the scene are blurred by an atmospheric haze that transforms the image into a semiabstract composition of lights and darks. Stella's view of the snow-clad Sixteenth Street Bridge spanning the Allegheny recalls such etchings by Whistler as *Old Putney Bridge* or *Old Battersea Bridge*, in which the buildings and bridges of the Thames were reduced to shadowy, abstract forms with soft edges and no details, arranged in asymmetric compositions that call to mind Japanese prints.

Whistler's prints depicting streets in Chelsea also come to mind as Stella's early drawings of city storefronts are considered. Even more directly reminiscent of Whistler's prints are such drawings as *The Hole in the Wall (Painter's Row: Dark Bedroom)* (see fig. 48), in which a composition of dark, abstract forms focuses on a small, brightly lit view through a doorway, recalling such quiet, intimate scenes as *The Kitchen* and *Nocturne, Furnace*.[40]

Similarly, the nocturnal theme seems to have held special appeal for Stella, who repeated it in his pastel compositions (figs. 55–59). Like Whistler's, some of Stella's nocturnes are among his most abstract compositions, in which the artist paid special attention to the effects of light penetrating darkness. In the Toledo *Nocturne* (see fig. 57), for example, light appears to glow from within the composition, muted by the matte colors of the pastel surface.[41] Unlike the night scenes in Stella's three major paintings of the teens and early 1920s—*Battle of Lights, Coney Island*; *Brooklyn Bridge*; and *The Voice of the City of New York Interpreted*—in which artificial, electric light illuminates the scene, his nocturnes on paper emphasize the mysterious, poetic qualities of light penetrating darkness, softening edges and transforming mundane forms into lyrical abstractions.

Pastels allowed Stella the freedom of drawing directly with color while providing him with the immediacy of expression he craved. The soft, rich, powdery surface of a pastel drawing appealed to him over the course of his

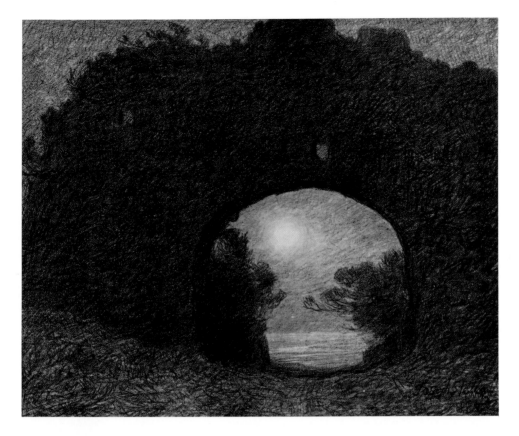

Figure 55

Nocturne, ca. 1900–1909
Charcoal
9 x 11 in.
Private collection

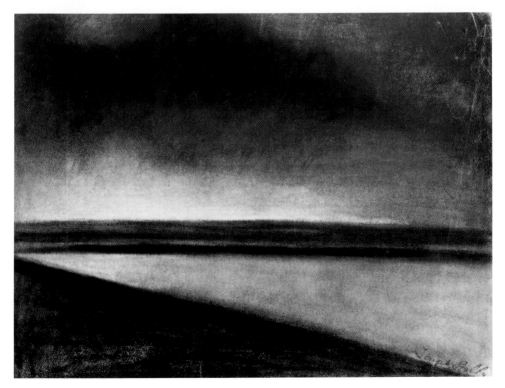

Figure 56

Nocturne, ca. 1917–18
Pastel
18 x 24 in. (approx.)
Columbus Museum of
Art, Ohio, Museum
Purchase, Howald Fund

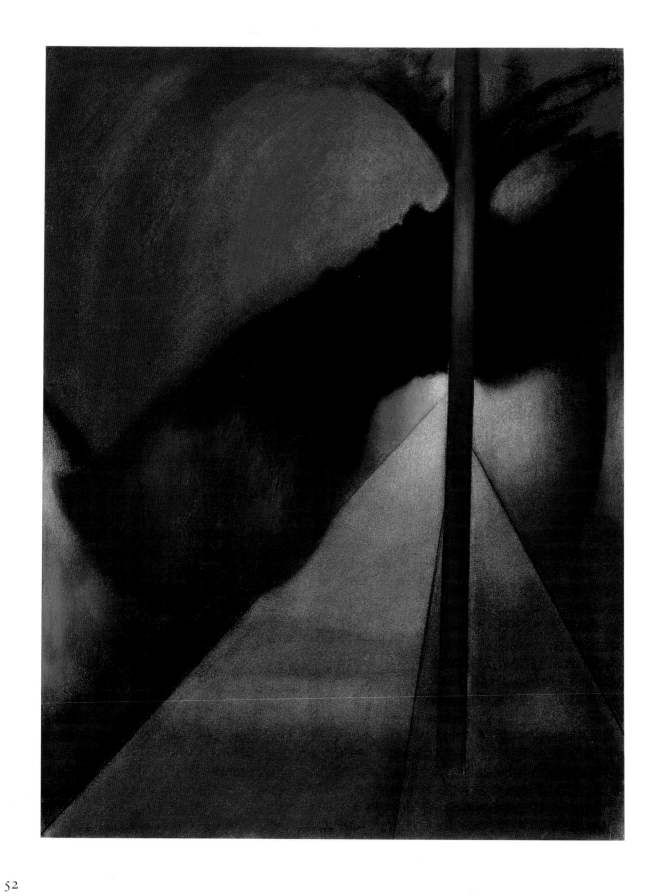

52

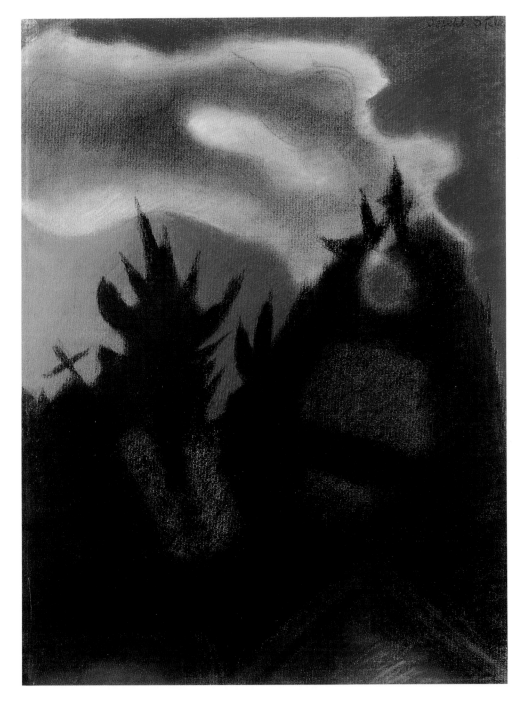

Figure 57

(far left)

Nocturne, ca. 1918

Pastel

23¼ x 17¹⁵⁄₁₆ in.

The Toledo Museum of

Art, Museum Purchase

Fund

Figure 58

Nocturne

Pastel

24 x 18 in.

Private collection

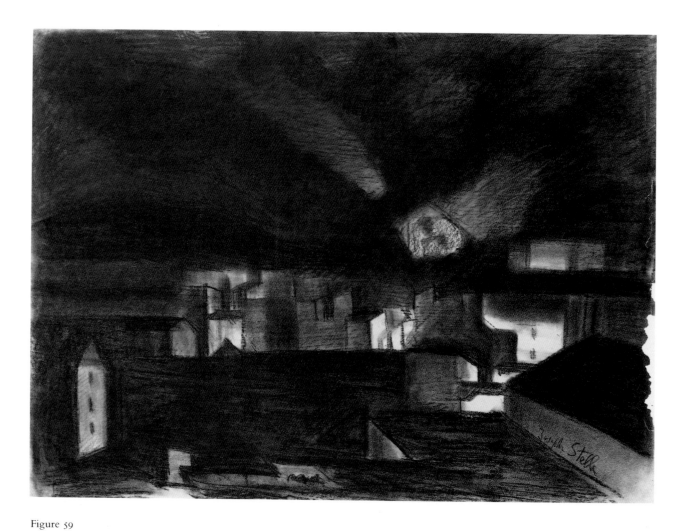

Figure 59

Nocturne, ca. 1930
Pastel
24½ x 33¼ in.
Modern Art Museum of
Fort Worth, Gift of Mr.
and Mrs. Edward R.
Hudson, Jr.

life as an artist, lending his many works in this medium a muted, atmospheric effect despite his frequent use of bright and varied colors. Poetic and evocative, Stella's pastel drawings suggest that important aspects of the Tonalist aesthetic continued to inspire his artistic imagination throughout his career.

Tonalism dominated American art in the 1880s and 1890s through the work of such artists as Whistler, Thomas Dewing, George Inness, Dwight Tryon, and Alexander Wyant, all of whom exhibited regularly in New York. Although now considered to be a conservative expression of nineteenth-century Romanticism, at the turn of the century Tonalism was in the vanguard of American painting and would have struck a harmonious chord in the poetic, idealistic nature of the young Stella.

Although Stella's specifically Tonalist drawings seem to be limited to his early years before his trip to Europe in 1909, many of the ideas and values associated with the Tonalist aesthetic persisted throughout his career. His propensity for drawing people in quiet, intimate poses—sleeping, relaxing on a park bench, or reading a book—reflects the preference of Whistler and other late nineteenth-century artists for moments of contemplation, reverie, or introspection that removed a figure from direct engagement with the surroundings. His tendency to idealize and abstract form can be traced as much to the antirealist bias of the Tonalists as to his discovery of Postimpressionism and modernist abstraction during his visit to Paris in 1911–12. The Tonalists' synthesis of the material and spiritual in nature, the poetic and evocative nature of their expression, and the sense of nostalgia and loss that often pervaded their work characterized Stella's sensibility and expression as well, even as his art moved away from the misty atmosphere and muted colors of his early landscapes.[42]

Similarly, the strictly tonal manner of his early depictions of heads and figures removes the sitters from the everyday world of surface appearances (fig. 60). Flattening the forms into abstract patterns, Stella distilled from the image not the facial characteristics that distinguish the sitter's nationality or individual appearance, as he did in his drawings of immigrants, but instead captured the timeless spirit beneath the external surface. When drawing a head or figure, "he always started with the eyes. He claimed the eyes were the soul of the person and should be seized at once."[43] Despite his more naturalistic rendering, Stella shared with the late nineteenth-century Tonalist and Symbolist artists the desire to convey a heightened sense of spiritual awareness in such an intense study as *Face of an Elderly Person* (fig. 61).

Figure 60

Man Resting,
ca. 1900–1905
Pencil
8 x 5½ in.
Linda and Louis Kaplan

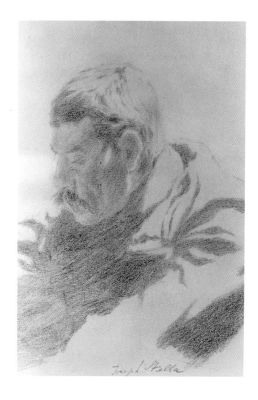

Figure 61

Face of an Elderly Person,
ca. 1907
Chalk
10¹⁄₁₆ x 7⅞ in.
Albert Keck

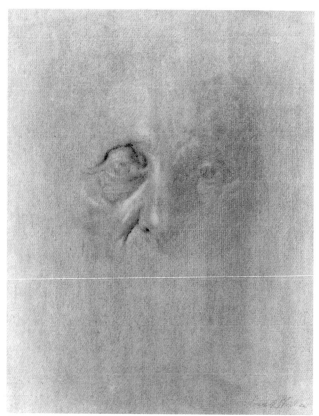

An even more immediate influence on Stella's tonal drawings of Pittsburgh may have been the 1908 exhibition of the Photo-Secession at the National Arts Club, in which the soft-focus, atmospheric photographs of Alfred Stieglitz, Edward Steichen, Clarence White, and Gertrude Kasebier were hung next to paintings.[44] The mood of quiet, intimacy, mystery, and suggestiveness they sought to achieve in their photographs directly contradicted the prevailing opinions of photography as mechanical and imitative, much as Stella's Tonalist drawings of Pittsburgh from the same year challenge the journalistic tradition of illustration. Like the Pictorialist photographers, Stella chose moments when the natural circumstances of a scene, such as a snowfall, fog, or dusk, contributed to the soft, atmospheric depiction, transforming an otherwise mundane, even unpleasant subject into an evocative, poetic statement.

A Romantic Visionary in the Modernist Tradition

Stella was already in his early thirties before he came into direct contact with the modernist art movements in Paris in 1911–12. Unlike other artists who first visited Paris during their formative years, he was no longer a young student but was already a mature artist who would exhibit three works in the 1912 Salon des Indépendants. Although Stella readily adopted many of the formal innovations to which he was exposed during his sojourn in Paris, he did not reject out of hand the legacy of the past. Instead, he synthesized a dynamic personal expression that had its roots in the nineteenth century and saw its flowering in the twentieth.

The formal innovations of the vanguard art movements represented for Stella a new language with which to express more intensely and directly many of the aesthetic concerns he had acquired over the course of his life and career. Like other important American modernist artists such as Arthur Dove and Marsden Hartley, Stella translated the late nineteenth-century romantic visionary tradition into a dynamic modernist idiom in which the symbolic content of the work remained an intrinsic element of the artist's expressive concerns.

Above all, Stella valued freedom, and the discoveries he made in Paris opened his eyes to possibilities he had not previously recognized:

What excited me most was the vista in front of me . . . the panorama of the most hyperbolic chromatic wealth. No more inhibition of any kind . . . but full adventure into a virgin forest of thrilling visions, heralded by alluring vivid colors, resonant as explosions of joy, the vermilion, green, violet, and orange high notes soaring upon the most luscious deep tonalities. To feel absolutely free to express this adventure was a bliss and rendered painting a joyful source, spurring the artist to defy and suffer any hardship in order to obtain his goal.[45]

Stella's introduction to the expressive possibilities offered by Fauvism and Futurism came just after he had realized the futility of trying to recapture the styles and techniques of the past during his sojourn in Italy. The new vocabulary of form and color revealed to him in Paris stirred the core of his poetic imagination with the thrill of discovery and the romance of rebellion.

With the enthusiasm of a convert, Stella adopted a Postimpressionist palette soon after his stay in Paris, and by 1913 he had mastered the dynamism of Futurist abstraction, doubtless under the influence of the landmark Futurist exhibition at Galerie Bernheim-Jeune in February 1912. His paintings of the following decade include some of the most radical and celebrated departures from his earlier work, further reinforcing the perception that he had broken with the past to assume a leadership role in the vanguard of American modernist painting. More important than a mere stylistic transformation in Stella's work, his exposure to the modernist art movements in Paris, reinforced by the experience of the Armory Show in New York in 1913, stimulated an important change of approach to his subject matter. Eschewing the strong reliance on observation that characterized his pre-Paris works, as well as the analytical emphasis of Cubism, Stella came to rely heavily on his imagination as the source of his imagery:

Cubism and Futurism interest me to a very great degree. Although they resemble in many ways from an exterior point of view and they both strive for some similar points, they are apart in many ways. Cubism is static. Futurism is dynamic. Cubism tries to find and finds its descendence in the work of some of the old masters. Futurism strives to be absolutely free of any tradition: its effort chiefly lies in creating a new sort of language apt to express the feelings and emotions of the modern artist.[46]

At the core of his bold new expression lay the soul of a romantic visionary, who had expanded the scope and power of his creative vocabulary through his contact with Fauvism, Cubism, and Futurism, but who still maintained many of the values and aesthetic sensibilities of late nineteenth-century art and literature. The subjective iconography and antimaterialist concerns of the Symbolist poets and painters of the late nineteenth century emerged more overtly in Stella's work after his trip to Paris. Although the muted tonalities and misty atmospheric effects of his pre-Paris compositions gave way to the vibrant colors and dynamic compositions of his Futurist-inspired paintings, Stella continued to express a poetic interpretation of his surroundings, a fundamental desire to evoke a mood, and a heightened sense of spiritual awareness. He prolonged for yet one more generation the nineteenth century's romantic search for the beautiful and the sublime in nature, expanding the scope of his inspiration to urban and industrial imagery as well.

Because of the strong impact that Stella's experiences in Paris had on his stylistic development, it has been assumed that Paris had freed Stella from the past. Stella himself interpreted his own development after returning to New York from Paris as a radical break with the past: "The bandages of stale prejudices torn from my eyes, the shackles of every school broken, I was in full possession of a great freedom of movement to start off the race through new fields that opened before me."[47]

Stella's best-known paintings, created in the years following his stay in Paris, are characterized by the abstracted forms, dynamic line, and intense colors inspired by his contact with Fauvism and Futurism. His *Battle of Lights, Coney Island* (fig. 62) might arguably be considered the most fully developed Futurist painting by an American artist, and his impressive *Brooklyn Bridge* (see fig. 28) has assumed almost iconic significance as a symbol of America's dynamism and industrial prowess. *The Voice of the City of New York Interpreted* (see fig. 29) has been characterized as "the most important painting of Stella's career, and one of the most exhilarating American works of the early modern period."[48] On the strength of these monumental compositions, Stella's fame as the leading American Futurist and his place in the history of American modernist art were determined. Attracted to the optimism and vitality that Futurism proclaimed, to its concern with contemporary life and urban subject matter, and probably to its Italian origins as well, Stella adopted it as the style best suited to express the dynamism of modern life. In many of his major paintings between 1913 and 1921, Stella adopted numerous stylistic devices associated with Futurist painting: the illusion of motion, urban subject matter, abstracted form and color, diagonal lines of force, interpenetrating planes, and overall sense of dynamism. His allegiance

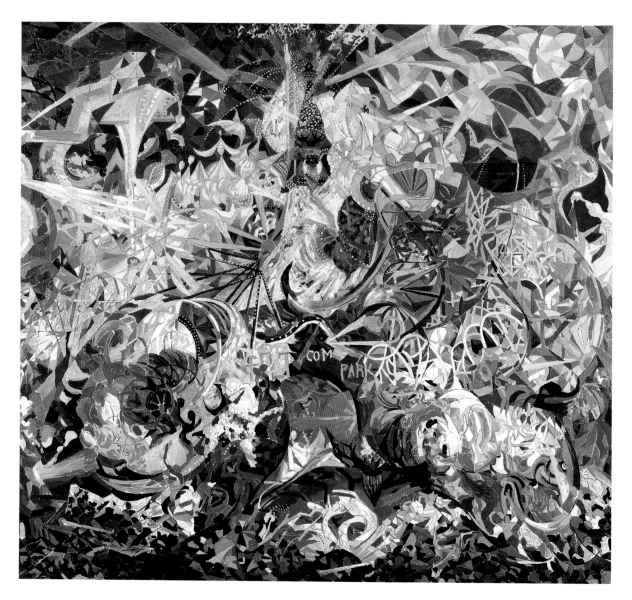

Figure 62

*Battle of Lights, Coney
Island*, ca. 1913
Oil on canvas
76 x 84 in.
Yale University Art
Gallery, New Haven,
Connecticut, Gift of
Collection Société
Anonyme

to the movement, however, had less to do with the formal precepts that enriched his expressive vocabulary than with the Futurists' mystical identity between object and emotion, their aspiration to incorporate the perception of all the senses into a single image, their "effort to kindle magic in an unmysterious world."[49]

His commitment to Futurism was relatively short-lived; he was uncomfortable with the bombastic nationalism, overt militarism, and wholesale rejection of tradition propounded by various Futurist manifestoes.[50] As early as 1913 he publicly declared his independence from its dogma: "[One must] paint sincerely without trying to please the Futurists or the Post-Impressionists or to displease the Academicians."[51] He felt free to choose only those aspects of Futurist expression that were meaningful to him and to ignore or reject the others.

Around 1916, when Stella moved to Brooklyn to teach Italian in a Baptist seminary, he entered a period of introspection and spiritual renewal. During this time he meditated and read his favorite poets.[52] Smarting from public criticism of his most important painting to date, *Battle of Lights, Coney Island*, in *The Evening Sun*, as well as from the loss of his brother's financial support, Stella recognized an opportunity to reorient his work toward a more personal expression: "Brooklyn gave me a sense of liberation. The vast view of her sky, in opposition to the narrow one of NEW YORK, was a relief—and at night, in her solitude, I used to find, intact, the green freedom of my own self."[53] Despite the upheaval and anxiety engendered by World War I and the responsibility of supporting himself, Stella entered the most creative and productive phase of his career.

Central to Stella's work from the period of approximately 1916 to 1922 is his attempt to invest the material world with spiritual significance and to create a symbolic language of form with which to express his personal fantasies, dreams, and visions. During the years immediately following his return from Paris, Stella had explored the formal qualities of line and color, in some of the most completely abstract works of his entire career (fig. 63). Relying heavily on watercolor and ink, materials that encouraged fluidity and spontaneity, Stella pushed the limits of Futurist dynamism toward total abstraction (figs. 64, 65).

Although there is no documentation that Stella was familiar with the paintings or writings of Wassily Kandinsky as early as 1913, his search for spiritual content in art through color and abstract form suggests that he was. In the July 1912 issue of *Camera Work*, Alfred Stieglitz published translated

Figure 63

Abstraction, ca. 1914
Watercolor
11¾ x 7¾ in.
Mr. and Mrs. Michael
M. Rea

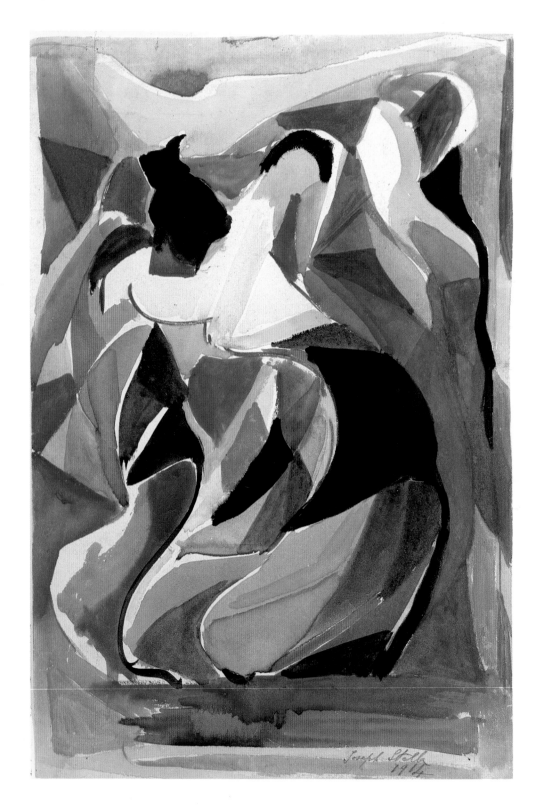

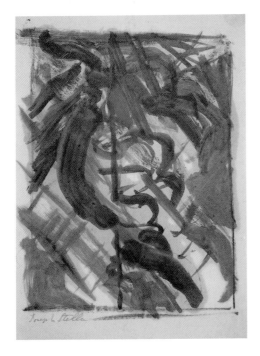

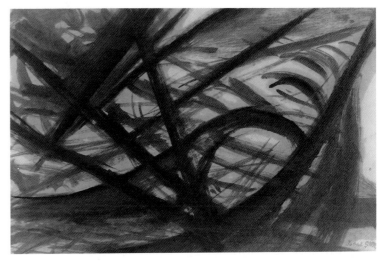

Figure 64

Composition, ca. 1913–15
Watercolor and oil
7⅞ x 5⅞ in.
Collection, The Museum
of Modern Art, New
York, Gift of Larry
Aldrich

Figure 65

Futurist Study, 1915
Ink
5¾ x 8⅞ in.
Albright-Knox Art
Gallery, Buffalo, George
Cary Fund, 1975

extracts from Kandinsky's *On the Spiritual in Art.* Stella did not return from Europe until the end of 1912, but the issue would have been available to him, especially at the time he saw Kandinsky's *Improvisation No. 27* in the Armory Show early in 1913. This article introduced many young American artists to Kandinsky, and the first complete English translation of *Uber das Geistige in der Kunst* appeared in 1914 under the title *The Art of Spiritual Harmony.* By 1914 Kandinsky had attracted so much attention in the American art world that one could learn of his ideas simply by reading the newspaper.[54]

The expressive content of the work of art remained Stella's main concern, and he began to develop and codify a vocabulary of form and color with which to communicate the visions of his inner eye and romantic soul and his spiritual aspirations:

Many nights I stood on the [Brooklyn] bridge—and in the middle alone—lost—a defenceless [*sic*] prey to the surrounding swarming darkness—crushed by the mountainous black impenetrability of the skyscrapers—here and there lights resembling suspended falls of astral bodies or fantastic splendors of remote rites—I felt deeply moved, as if on the threshold of a new religion or in the presence of a new DIVINITY.[55]

Standing alone on the bridge, in the middle of the night, Stella "opened himself to the rhythmic patterns of this vast, synthetic landscape in much the same way that a Romantic poet a century earlier opened himself to nature."[56]

According to Carlo de Fornaro, Stella's first youthful ambition was to become a poet, not a painter.[57] Even before Stella arrived in the United States as a young immigrant, he had already developed sincere admiration for Walt Whitman and Edgar Allan Poe, whose poetry and ideas continued to inspire him throughout his career, perhaps more profoundly and consistently than any visual art movement or artist. Charmion von Wiegand, an acquaintance of Stella's, recalled that he could quote endlessly from Whitman and Poe.[58] It was through their eyes that Stella viewed New York after his return from Europe in 1912 and later conceived his monumental *Brooklyn Bridge*:

> To realize this towering imperative vision in all its integral possibilities I lived days of anxiety, torture, and delight alike, trembling all over with emotion as those railings in the midst of the bridge vibrating at the continuous passage of the trains. I appealed for help to the soaring verse of Walt Whitman and to the fiery Poe's plasticity.[59]

The drama and spirituality of their poetry provided a model for Stella to reconcile the evils of industrialism, of which he was well aware from his experiences in Monongah and Pittsburgh, with the glories of industrial progress, as symbolized by the Brooklyn Bridge. Inspired by the optimistic romanticism of Whitman and the Symbolist imagery of Poe, Stella summoned his own poetic imagination to create the visual equivalent of their poetry, transforming the realities and contradictions of machine-age society into a visionary expression that transcended the viewer's sensory or intellectual perception.

A disciple of Ralph Waldo Emerson, Whitman insisted on an art based on contemporary life that used a symbolic language. As defined by Emerson, the role of the artist was essentially spiritual. The artist was not to be a reporter who faithfully transcribes the realities of society, but a prophet and reformer who projects an idealized interpretation of experience that could in turn serve as an inspiration and guide to others.[60] In Whitman's poetry, Stella saw the path to the future, in which nature and industry, progress and spirituality, reality and beauty could all be united through poetic imagination.

Stella endowed the industrial forms of his urban environment with the power to represent invisible forces and sublime experience:

Meanwhile the verse of Walt Whitman . . . soaring above as a white aeroplane of Help . . . was leading the sails of my Art through the blue vastity of Phantasy, while the telegraph wires, trembling around, as if expecting to propagate a new musical message, like aerial guides leading to Immensity, were keeping me awake with an insatiable thirst for new adventures.[61]

In the *Telegraph Pole,* the tall, centralized image assumes iconic significance as a link between the material and spiritual worlds that Stella wished to bridge (fig. 66). The diagonal wires converging on a single point at once recall the diagonal force lines in Futurist painting as well as Renaissance illustrations of linear perspective. In his many renditions of the Brooklyn Bridge, from quick sketches to finished paintings, the powerful cables echo the forms of the telegraph wires as symbolic manifestations of his metaphysical inner vision. Stella's images of American industrial civilization challenge the imaginative capacity of the human mind to integrate rational and mystical experience.

Conversely, Poe denied the power of art to uplift, to inculcate a moral. Instead, he subscribed to the "art for art's sake" philosophy that the proper province of art was the expression of beauty, especially divine beauty. In Poe's mind, poetry—and by extension, all works of art—should be efflorescent and impassioned, in contrast to the cool, precise language called for by the intellectual tract. He believed that the poetic evocation of mood should be based on the suggestive and metaphysical rather than the factual and descriptive.[62]

While Whitman influenced Stella's enthusiastic embrace of urban and industrial imagery, it was the dramatic imagination and Symbolist imagery of Poe that revealed to Stella a means to infuse this imagery with the drama, mystery, and passion of his inner vision:

New meanings dash out of his unexpected chromatic blending. The Medusa of Mystery leaps to light with a new physiognomy: new aspects are revealed, new enigmatic blazing hieroglyphics are shrieked by thunder and lightning in livid upheavals of earth and sky.

One moves, breaths uplifted to a superhuman atmosphere, to the regions where the candor of the domes elevated by Art perpetually radiate against the flaming gold of eternity, where everything becomes redeemed with the transfiguration practiced by abstraction. . . . Poe, using abstraction, remains, till our day, the point of departure of all the glorious modern French literature.[63]

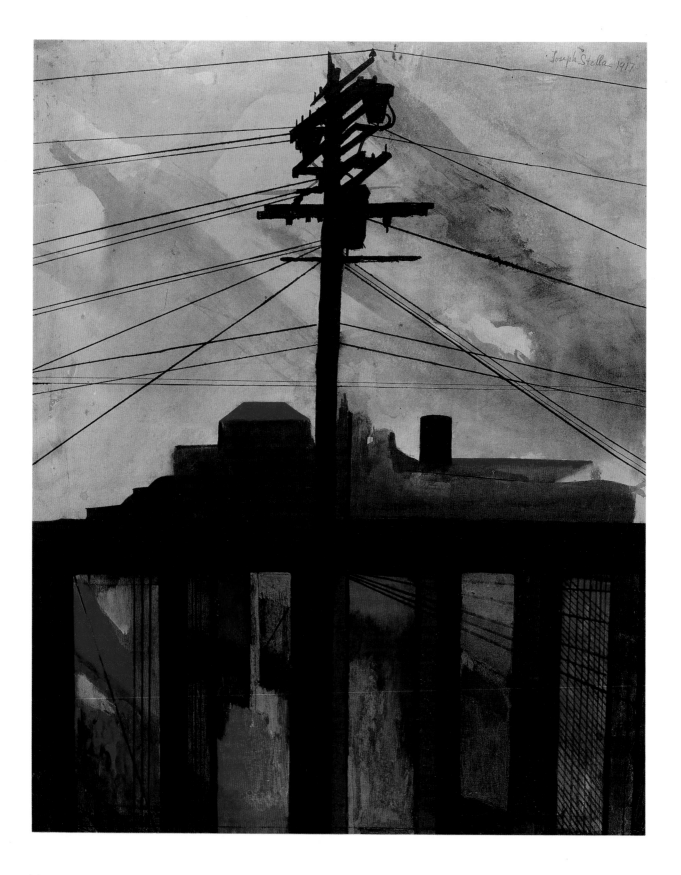

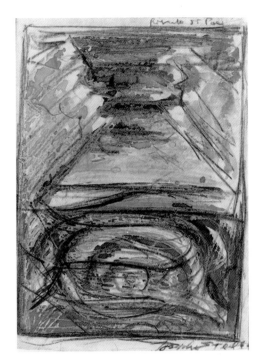

Figure 66

(far left)

Telegraph Pole, 1917

Gouache

25⅛ x 19¾ in.

Mr. and Mrs. Meyer P.

Potamkin

Figure 67

Portrait of Poe

Watercolor and crayon

20½ x 15½ in.

(appprox.)

Mrs. Gloria Gurney

In abstract symbolism Stella discerned the principles to which he aspired: the triumph of imagination over observation, spiritual expression over material concerns, the sensory over the intellectual, as well as the seamless fusion of music, poetry, drama, and the visual arts into a purely subjective synthesis (fig. 67).

The Drama of American Industry

Approximately ten years after he created the delicate, tonal, moody, and mysterious views of Pittsburgh for *The Survey* magazine, he returned to industrial subject matter with renewed passion and drama.[64]

> War was raging with no end to it . . . so it seemed. There was a sense of awe, of terror weighing on everything. . . . Opposite my studio a huge factory . . . its black walls scarred with red stigmas of mysterious battles . . . was towering with the gloom of a prison. At night fires gave to innumerable windows menacing blazing looks of demons. . . . Smoke, perpetually arising, perpetually reminded of war.[65]

At least two of the new series of drawings were based closely on photographs published in "The Pittsburgh Survey" (6 March 1909) (figs. 68–70), while other drawings were based on Stella's surroundings in Brooklyn, a visit to Bethlehem, Pennsylvania, and possibly a return visit to Pittsburgh in 1918 in conjunction with another commission for *The Survey* magazine.[66]

Inspired by the simultaneous horror and devastation of World War I, Stella transformed the mundane panorama of an industrial landscape into starkly elegant compositions whose powerful, dark, abstract forms loom grandly, albeit somewhat menacingly, against an austere horizon (fig. 71). The soft textures and rich tonalities of charcoal and pastel soften the smooth, geometrized lines and forms and impart to the scenes a mysterious, other-worldly atmosphere. The dramatic red and orange sky of *Night Fires* intensifies the emotional impact of the composition with its allusion to the simultaneous creative and destructive power of fire (fig. 72). Stella's coal ovens and storage tanks conjure the tremendous forces at work in the modern world that shape the destinies of people and nations.

The bold compositions and monumental forms of these drawings anticipate the industrial themes and architectonic structures favored by the Precisionists during the 1920s and 1930s. Stella's early synthesis of realism and abstraction, however, was directed toward a subjective, romantic interpretation of his subject while the more classical, formalist compositions of "Cubist-Realism" involved a more objective, analytical approach.[67] As he trans-

Figure 68

Mountains of Ore in Ore Yard at Blast Furnace, ca. 1908

Photograph reproduced in *The Survey* 21 (6 March 1909)

Whereabouts unknown

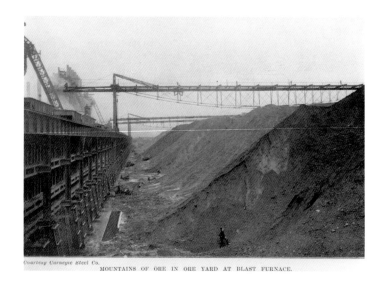

Courtesy Carnegie Steel Co.

MOUNTAINS OF ORE IN ORE YARD AT BLAST FURNACE.

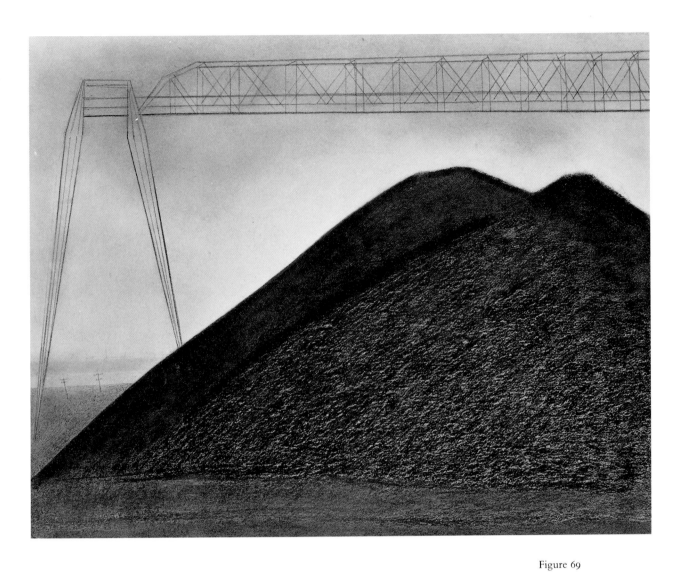

Figure 69

Coal Pile, ca. 1918–20
Charcoal
20 x 26 in.
The Metropolitan
Museum of Art, New
York, Arthur H. Hearn
Fund, 1950 (50.31.4)

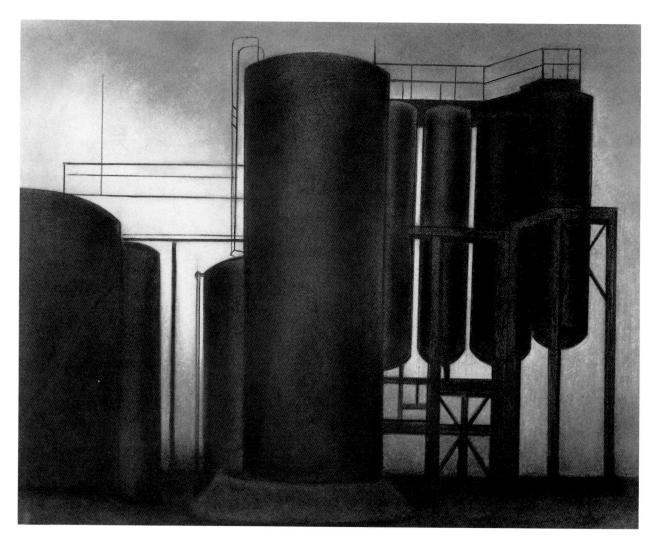

Figure 70

Tanks, ca. 1918–20
Charcoal
21⅞ x 28 in.
The Santa Barbara
Museum of Art,
California, Gift of
Wright Ludington

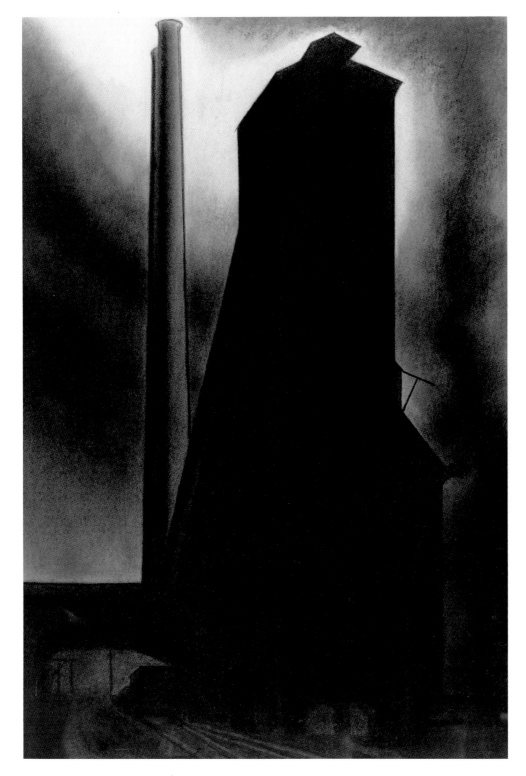

Figure 71

Grain Elevator,
ca. 1918–20
Charcoal
34¼ x 22⅞ in.
The Santa Barbara
Museum of Art,
California, Gift of
Wright Ludington

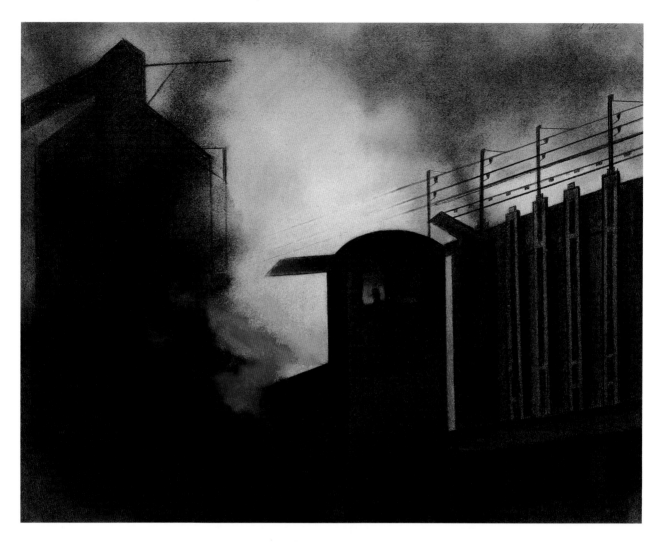

Figure 72

Night Fires, ca. 1918–20
Pastel
22½ x 29 in.
Milwaukee Art Museum,
Gift of Friends of Art

formed the generalized misty atmospheres of his earlier landscape drawings for *The Survey* into billowing plumes of smoke, or spectacular cloud formations, or abstract, serpentine forms, he invested the scene with a dramatic emotional charge, heightened by highlights of bright color (figs. 73, 74). Finding "beauty lying in the arabesque forms given by the structures of those huge volcano-like steel mills, emerging from the fluctuating waves of smoke and fog, with an eloquent mystery," Stella conceived analogies between the man-made creations and the forces of nature.[68]

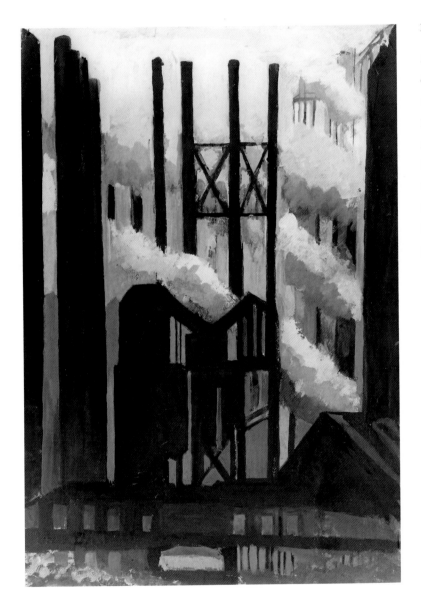

Figure 73

Steel Mill, ca. 1918–20
Gouache
17⅝ x 12⅜ in.
National Museum of
American Art,
Smithsonian Institution,
Washington, D.C.,
Given in memory of
Edith Gregor Halpert by
the Halpert Foundation

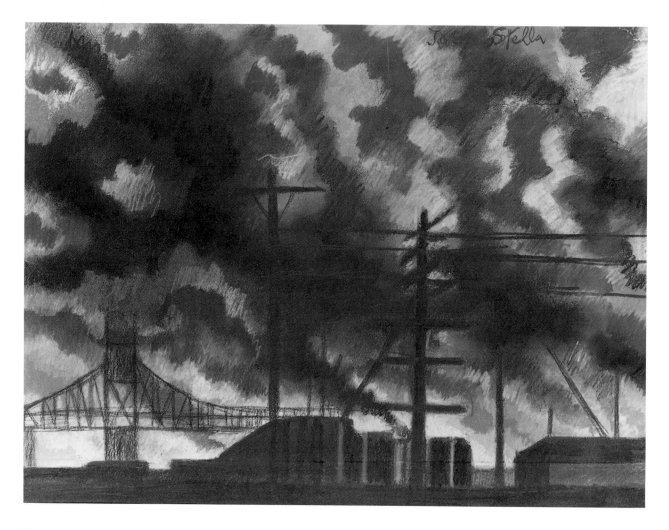

Figure 74

Pittsburgh, ca. 1918

Pastel

12 x 16½ in.

The Metropolitan

Museum of Art, New

York, Arthur H. Hearn

Fund, 1950 (50.31.5)

Macchine Naturali

The personal character of Stella's abstract symbolism is nowhere more evident than in a series of collages in which his conflicting sentiments about the old and the new, crafted and natural objects, formalist abstraction and expressive content, materialism and art find expression. Only two of the collages were ever reproduced in his lifetime, and there is no evidence that any of them were ever exhibited.[69] He made no reference to the collages in any of his writings, and he spoke very little about them, even to his closest friends.[70]

Created from the late teens through the mid 1940s, Stella's collages were composed from dirty, torn, shredded, wrinkled, or waterlogged bits of paper, leaves, wrappers, or other discarded materials. Possibly inspired by Kurt Schwitters's *Merz* collages, which were exhibited at the Société Anonyme in November and December 1920, Stella's collages retain a much more tangible sense of the actual materials from which they were created. Unlike Schwitters's compositions in which the bits of discarded paper are cut, torn, and arranged to create an overall design of planes, colors, and typography within a traditional rectangular or oval format, Stella focused more strongly on the individual scrap, its shape, texture, color, and unique character, which he emphasized by restricting the number of elements in a single composition. In further contrast to the pictorial and even decorative quality of Schwitters's collages, such stark compositions as *Collage #2* or *Macchina Naturale #12* (figs. 75, 76) emphasize the abstract, physical qualities of the materials. In the latter collage, the integrity of the white paper bag remains intact. Even in his more complex compositions, such as *Collage #17, Serenado*, the individual elements remain distinct and identifiable (fig. 77).

The spare, sensitively balanced compositions and careful attention to edges, textures, layers, colors, and relationships of abstract forms reveal strong formalist concerns. Such an approach, for its own sake, however, was anathema to Stella, and a careful consideration of the individual collage elements reveals a multilayered symbolism through which Stella expressed some of his most personal perceptions. In his later years Stella referred to his collages generically as *macchine naturali*, an expression that can be loosely translated as "natural constructions" (with mechanical or industrial overtones).[71] By integrating both natural and manufactured materials into a single image, Stella expressed his simultaneous attraction to the wonders of industrial progress and to the sublime forces and creations of nature, both of which claimed a powerful hold on his imagination.

Figure 75

Collage #2 (Green),
ca. 1921
Paper collage
12⅛ x 9⅛ in.
Modern Art Museum of
Fort Worth, The
Benjamin J. Tillar
Memorial Trust

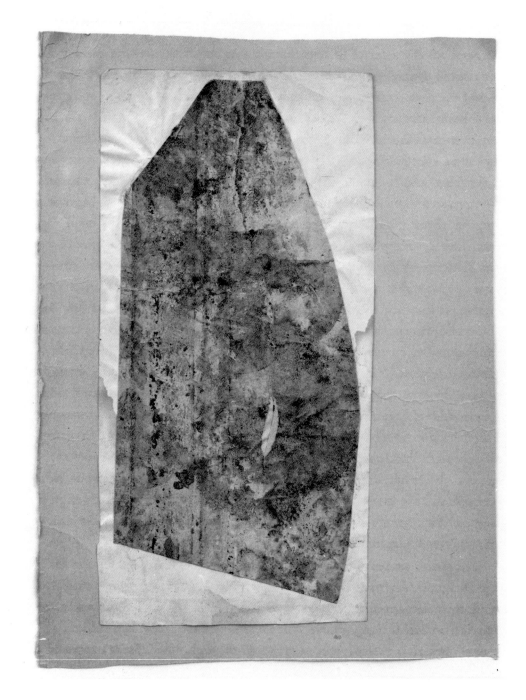

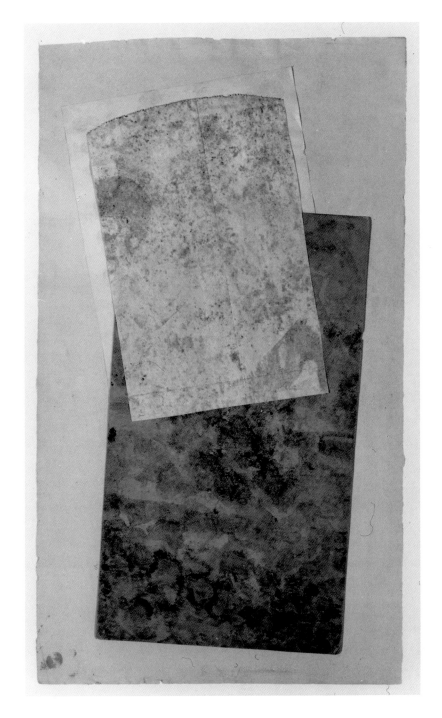

Figure 76

Macchina Naturale #12,
ca. 1922
Paper collage
17¼ x 10 in.
The Crispo Collection

Figure 77

Collage #17, Serenado
Paper collage
8½ x 6½ in.
Courtesy Salander
O'Reilley Galleries,
New York

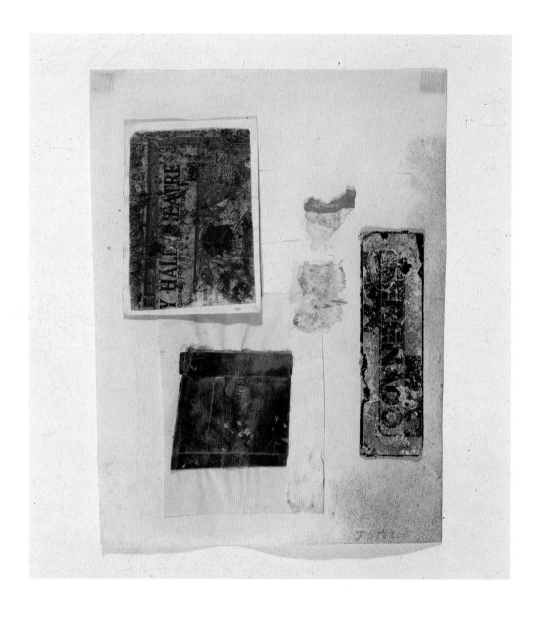

Paper itself acquires a symbolic meaning as a product created by the industrial transformation of the living fiber of a tree into an inanimate object, which assumes a life of its own as a paper bag (see fig. 76), cigarette wrapper, theater program (see fig. 77), envelope, or packing label (figs. 78–81). Used, discarded, or mutilated, the paper is subjected to the natural process of decay until the artist plucks it from the street and makes it part of a work of art.

The refined, subtle compositions assume a presence and preciousness that belies the lowly materials from which they are composed. A fabric of leaves, paper, sand, and wood in *Collage #11* becomes the natural equivalent of Duchamp's readymades, transformed from debris into art by the intervention of the artist (fig. 82). If Duchamp's urinal (*Fountain*, 1917) or snow shovel (*In Advance of the Broken Arm*, 1915) pay tribute to modern industrial design, Stella's readymades acknowledge the timeless forces of nature that ultimately subject all synthetic objects to the natural forces of decomposition and decay, with renewal and regeneration implicit in the process.

In his collages Stella recognizes both the positive and negative aspects of modern urbanization and technology, artistic tradition and innovation. His transformation of urban debris into something beautiful and precious affirms his faith in the power of art to supersede materialism, in the creative role of accident and inspiration. While the collages constitute the most radical, avant-garde work of his career, at the same time they also affirm his respect for old age and tradition. One recalls Stella's sketches of distorted or grotesque human features and the illustrations he provided for a 1905 article in *The Outlook* magazine, in which the artist portrays human dignity beneath the ugliness or crudeness of external appearances.[72] Scorned by many as the refuse of European civilization, immigrants, like street refuse, gained new stature and respect in Stella's art. Similarly, his fascination with the wrinkled and wizened faces of old men and continuing admiration for the Old Master tradition reveal a set of values at odds with the materialism, emphasis on youth and superficial appearance, isolationism, and wholesale rejection of tradition that made Stella uncomfortable with much of postwar American culture.

The scraps Stella chose for his collages often have important personal meaning for him. Theater tickets, theater programs, or pages from a French journal evoke nostalgia for another time and place. Scraps of his own writing appear in some (fig. 83). The Mecca tobacco wrapper, besides being an attractive design, recalls Stella's travels to North Africa (see fig. 78). Mecca,

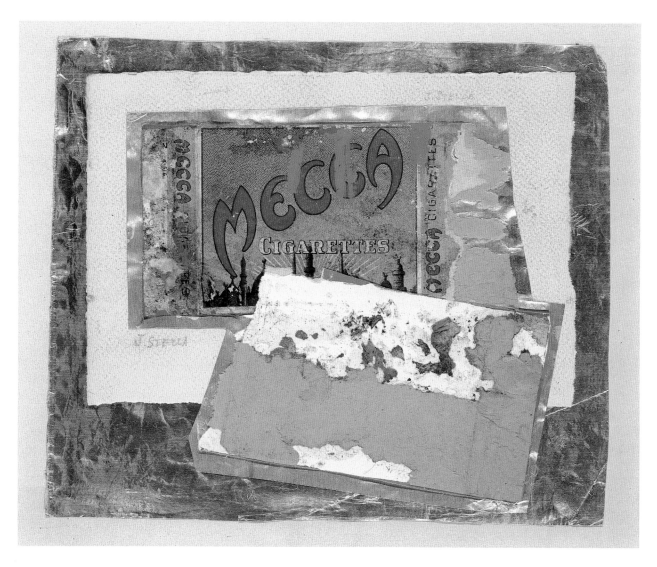

Figure 78

Mecca I
Collage of paper, tinfoil,
and tempera
13⅛ x 14¹⁵⁄₁₆ in.
National Museum of
American Art,
Smithsonian Institution,
Washington, D.C.

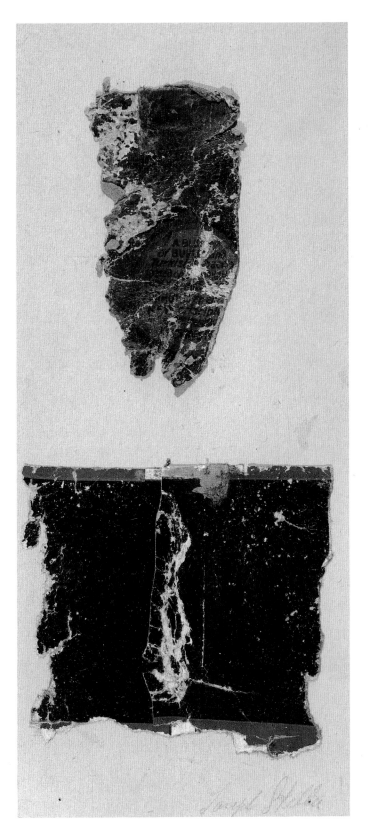

Figure 79

Black Descending
Paper collage
8 x 3½ in.
Jordan-Volpe Gallery,
Inc., New York

Figure 80

Collage #20, Red Seal
Collage of envelope,
paint, and paper
18 x 12 in.
Nancy Ellison and
Jerome Hellman

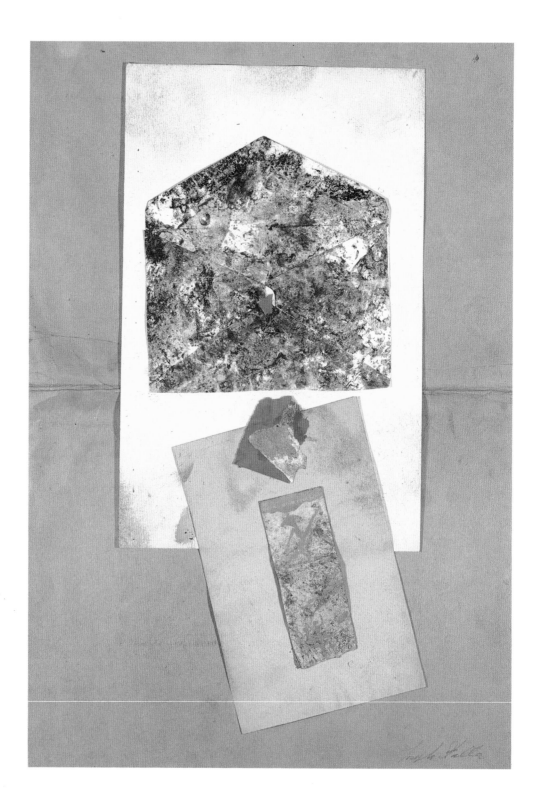

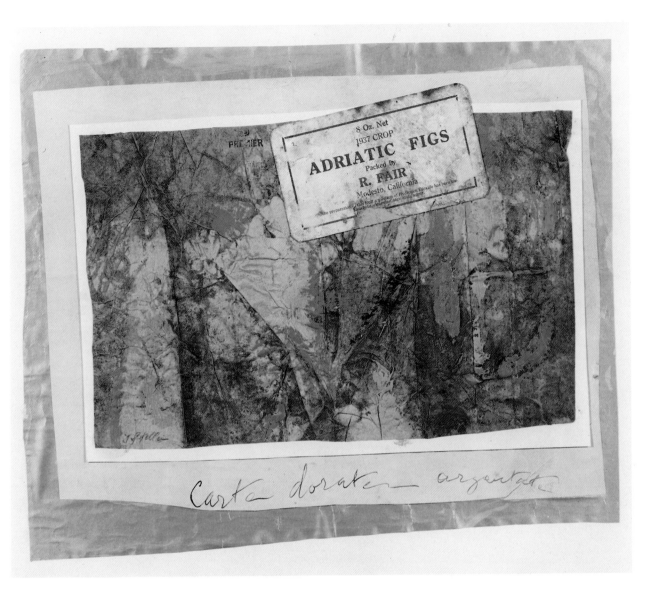

Figure 81

Adriatic Figs, ca. 1938
Collage of packing label
and paper
14 x 15^{15}/$_{16}$ in.
Collection of Whitney
Museum of American
Art, New York,
Gift of Mr. and Mrs.
Benjamin Weiss
(79.66.61)

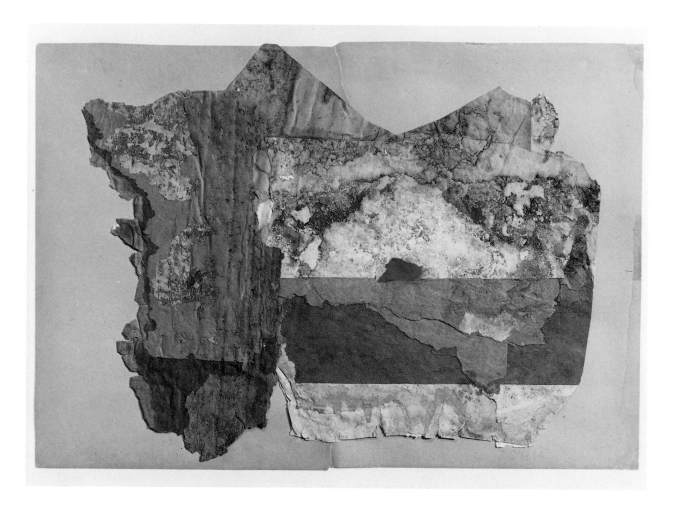

Figure 82

Collage #11
Collage of leaves, paper,
sand, and wood
11½ x 17 in.
Collection of Whitney
Museum of American
Art, New York,
Gift of Mrs. Morton
Baum (68.23)

as the holy city of Islam, also refers to Stella's spiritual concerns, as does his scrap of text from an article entitled "Mantegna As a Mystic" (fig. 84).[73]

His most unequivocal statement on war and materialism appears in a small, unusual collage in which one of his own drawings of a World War I soldier's head is mounted within a frame of dollar signs on a sheet of gold foil made in Japan (fig. 85). In his ironic memorial to "the war to end all wars," Stella seeks to reconcile the idealism of the cause with the death and profiteering that resulted. Reproductions of panels of his painting *New York Interpreted* figure prominently in several of his collages as if to reconcile his idealized vision of the city with the debris that he found in its streets (fig. 86).

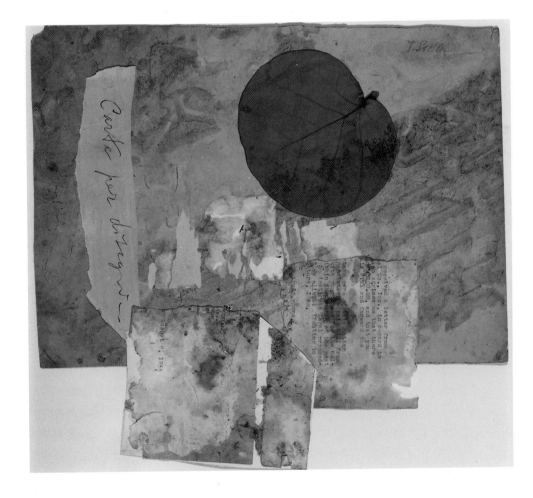

Figure 83

Macchina Naturale #9,
ca. 1936
Collage of leaf, paper,
and blue paint
11¾ x 13 in.
The Crispo Collection

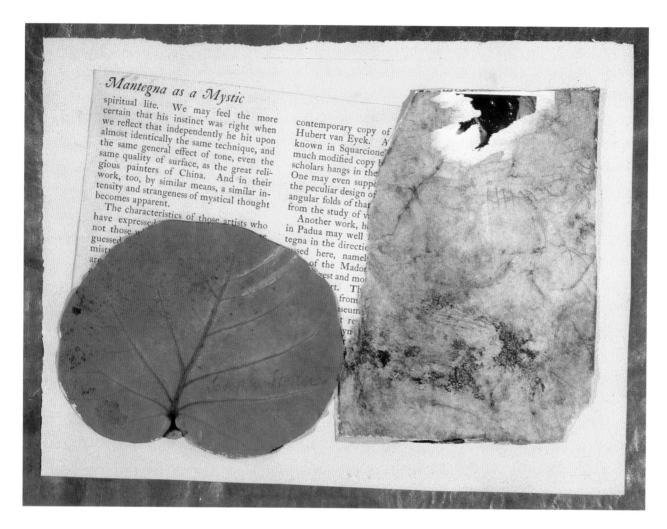

Figure 84

Untitled (Mantegna As a
Mystic)
Collage of leaf, magazine
scrap, and paper
10⅝ x 13⅜ in. (approx.)
David Nisinson

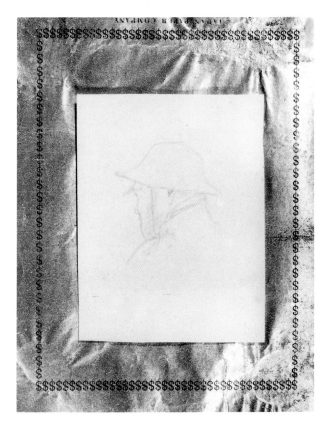

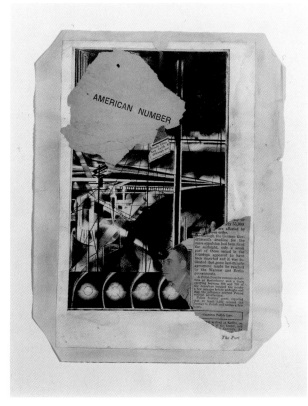

Figure 85

Untitled (World War I soldier)
Collage of pencil drawing and gold foil on gray paper
5½ x 4⅜ in.
Private collection

Figure 86

Macchina Naturale #18, ca. 1938
Collage of newspaper, photo reproduction, and paper
12⅜ x 9⅛ in.
The Crispo Collection

87

Visual "Poésie Pure"

In his collages, Stella infused the formal abstraction of modernist art movements with a highly evocative and complex personal symbolism. Relishing the freedom that a wide range of formal choices offered, Stella rejected consistency of style in favor of metaphorical expression, often adopting such Symbolist principles as analogy and correspondence, emotive color, contrast of opposites, and allusion to heighten the experience of mood, sensory experience, enigma, and mystery in his work. Symbolism allowed for a wide range of stylistic diversity, which is reflected in the lack of aesthetic coherence that characterizes Stella's oeuvre.

Symbolism had continued as an active concern well into the twentieth century both in Europe and the United States.[74] Because of the literary content and academic painting styles of many of its leading exponents, Symbolism has traditionally been considered as part of the conservative nineteenth-century tradition against which the early twentieth-century modernist movements reacted. In fact, Symbolism was very much alive in American modernist circles and found expression in the work of some of the leading abstract artists.[75] The accomplishments of such artists as Gauguin, Munch, Redon, Rodin, and Ryder were widely admired, and the Armory Show included many more Symbolist paintings than the more radical Fauve and Cubist works for which it is most notorious. The artist most comprehensively represented was Odilon Redon, who was featured in a miniretrospective of seventy-five paintings and prints. Symbolist writings were regularly reprinted in American publications, including *The Chap-Book*, featuring such writers as Maeterlinck, Mallarmé, and Verlaine. The American critic Charles Caffin, as well as others, wrote on Symbolism in Stieglitz's journal *Camera Work*. Even the popular press took notice of such modern visionaries as Charles Baudelaire, Joris-Carl Huysmans, Auguste Rodin, and Richard Wagner. Despite its ostensible rejection of past tradition, Futurism also retained a strong commitment to Symbolist principles, which Filippo Marinetti continued to propagate in Italy in his journal *Poesia*. The strong Symbolist content of Futurism was no doubt an important factor in Stella's attraction to this movement.

The critical role of color in Stella's paintings recalls the overwhelming impact that Postimpressionism had made on him in Paris. Stella had met Henri Matisse and visited his studio, and shortly after his return to New York, he recalled: "The color of Matisse haunted me for months: I could feel in it a great force and a great vitality not dreamed of."[76] In his most completely Futurist work, *Battle of Lights, Coney Island* (see fig. 62), Stella relied considerably on the evocative, sensory experience of color to suggest mood: "I used the intact purity of the vermilion to accentuate the carnal frenzy of the new bacchanal and all the acidity of the lemon yellow for the dazzling lights storming all around."[77] The dominant deep blue tonality in *Brooklyn Bridge* (see fig. 28), punctuated by areas of intense color, invokes the mystical qualities of night pierced by mystery of Poe's white light.

Color had assumed an expressive value for Stella closely akin to the vital connotative function of color in Symbolist verse.[78] In contrast to the more arbitrary color choices favored by the Fauves, Stella used color and light in an evocative manner to connote content by creating a mood through a chromatic equivalent: "One moved, breathed in an atmosphere of . . . the impending Drama of Poe's tales. . . . With anxiety I began to unfold all the poignant deep resonant colors, in quest of the chromatic language that would be the exact eloquence of steely architectures."[79]

The extraordinary group of pastel compositions that date from approximately 1917–1919 testify to the central importance that color had assumed for Stella around this time (figs. 87–90). Drawing with sticks of pure pigment, he was able to shade, blend, intensify, and superimpose color more freely and directly than watercolor or oil paint allowed.[80] Even in black-and-white charcoal drawings, black became a positive color—a departure from his more tonal use of the medium in earlier compositions (see fig. 71).

The central role of color in Stella's thinking is equally apparent in his description of another major painting of that period, *Tree of My Life* (fig. 91):

The pure cobalt with which our sky is covered lovingly protects and encloses, at the upper part of the canvas, the whiteness of the flowers that close off the last arduous flight of the Spiritual Life. And the pure beauty of our homeland . . . transformed, ennobled by the nostalgia of memories, flows all around like healthful air, joyfully animating the sumptuous floral orchestration that follows the episodes of the ascension with appropriate resounding chords: the clanging of silver and gold, signifying the first triumphs, and the deep adagio, played by the charged, rich greens and reds, loosened from the sudden searing cry of the intense vermilion of the lily, placed as a seal of generative blood at the base of the robust trunk twisted, already twisted by the first fierce struggles in the snares that Evil Spirits set on our path.[81]

Figure 87

Nativity, ca. 1917–18
Pastel
37 x 19⅛ in.
Collection of Whitney
Museum of American
Art, New York (31.469)

Figure 88

(far right)
Landscape
Pastel
22 x 17 in.
The Metropolitan
Museum of Art, New
York, Bequest of
Katherine S. Dreier, 1952
(53.45.4)

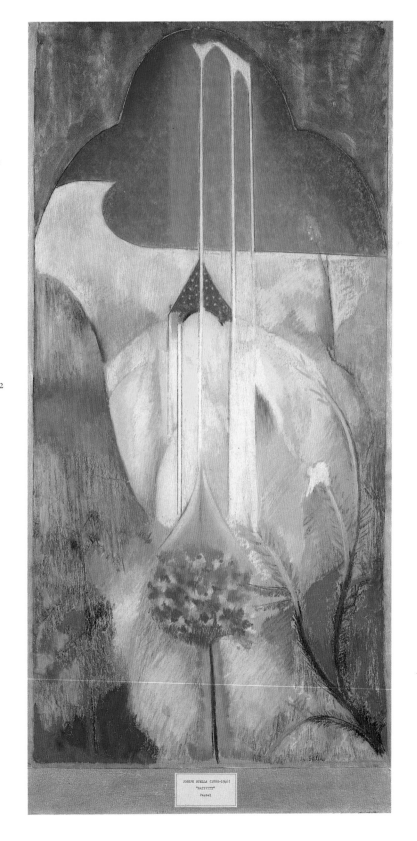

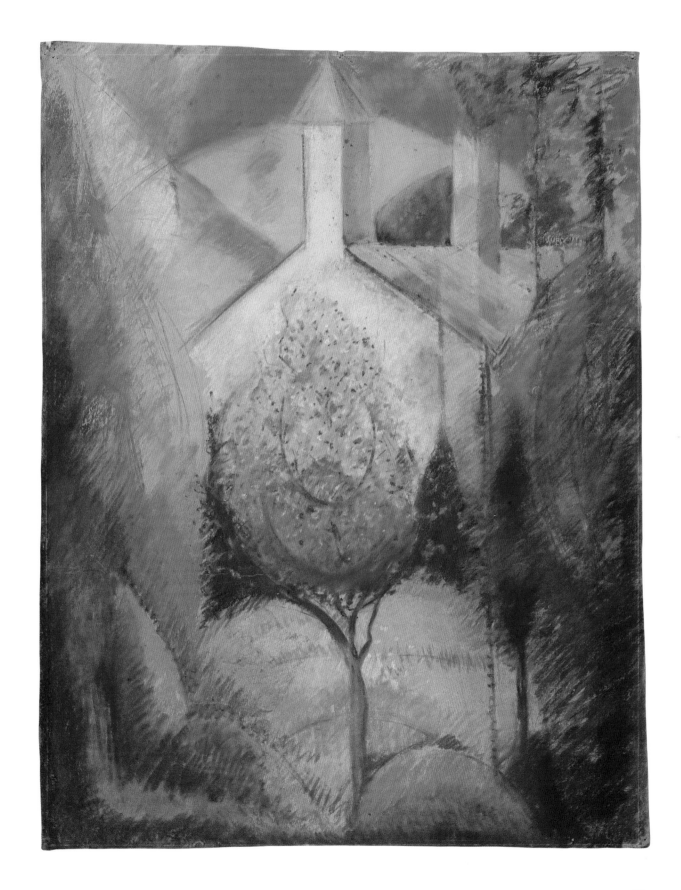

Figure 89

Abstraction (Waterlilies),
ca. 1917–18
Pastel and pencil
39¼ x 29¼ in.
The Newark Museum,
New Jersey, Gift of Mrs.
Rhoda Weintraub Ziff,
1983

Figure 90

(far right)
Pyrotechnic Fires, ca. 1919
Pastel
40 x 29½ in.
Harvey and Françoise
Rambach

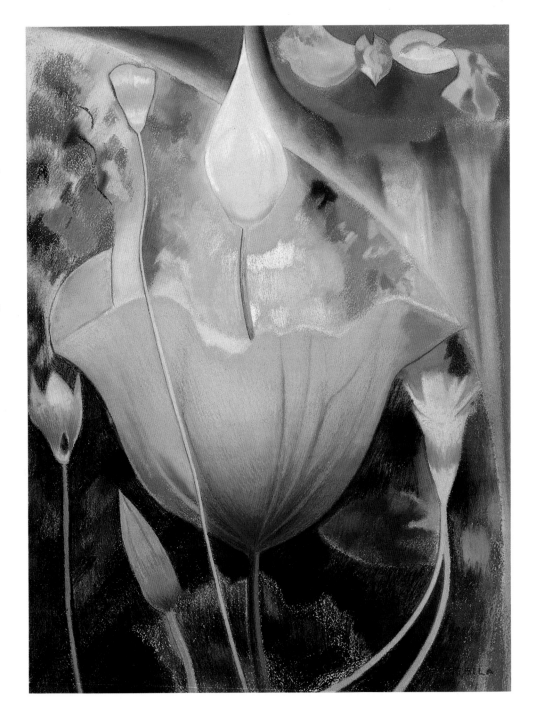

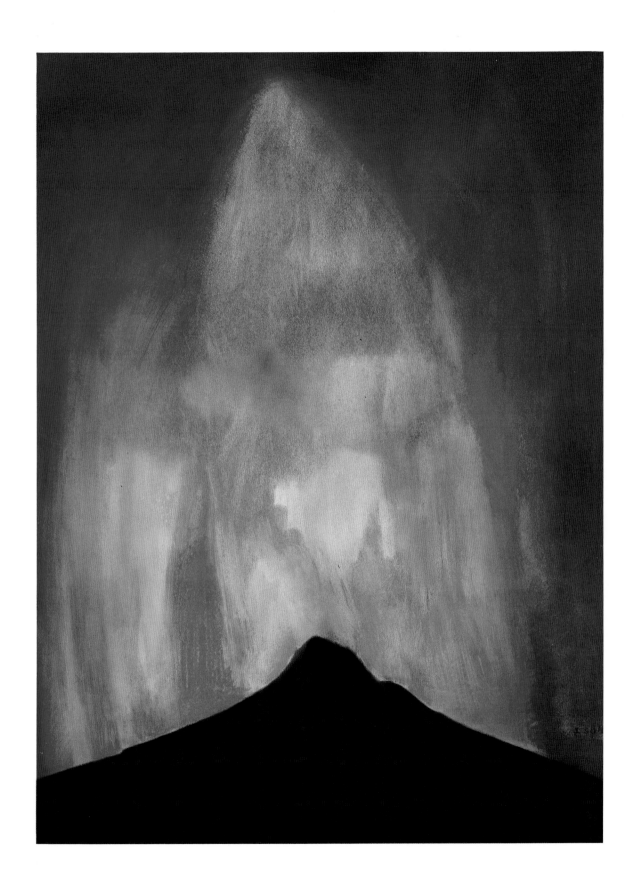

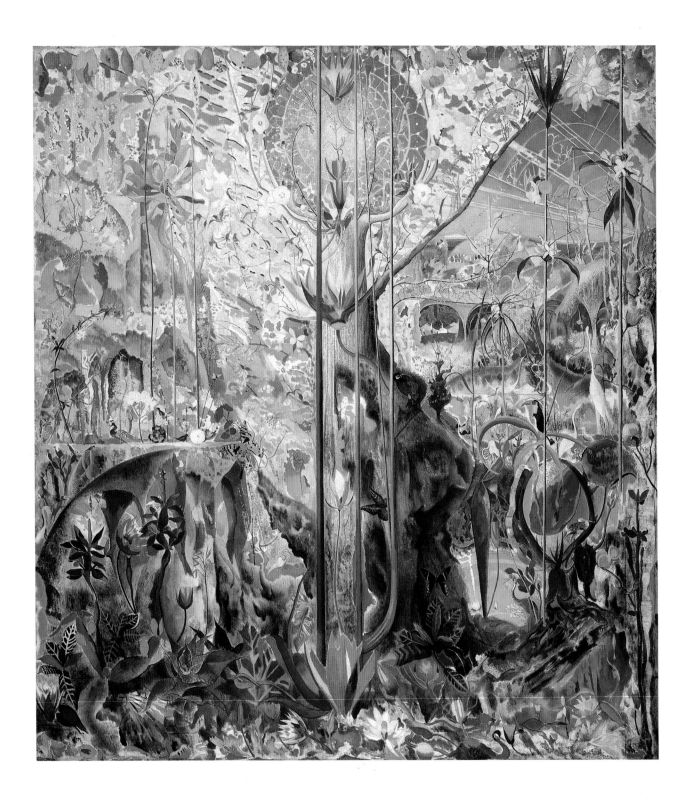

94

As in his Futurist works, Stella emphasized the decorative, symphonic arrangement of color and form, and he invoked the emotive power of concentrated color. Central to the expression of *Tree of My Life* is the simultaneous mood of joy and nostalgia evoked by the artist through color, light, and symbolic form.

Brooklyn Bridge and *Tree of My Life* may be seen—and indeed may well have been created—as companion pieces to express visually the contradictory impulses then preoccupying Stella in his art and personal life. The gnarled form of the tree trunk, animation and verticality of the profuse foliage, spiderweb intricacy of line, and halolike sun that transforms the central image into a quasi-religious icon function much like the arches, cables, and electric lights in Brooklyn Bridge.[82] Stella developed an elaborate metaphor based on the Symbolist principles of analogy and the contrast of opposites: the lily at the base of the tree trunk and the diamond at the fulcrum of the bridge composition, natural light and electric light, a network of powerful cables and delicate spiderwebs. In complementary images of day and night, artificial and natural forms, Stella explored his dual allegiance to America and Italy, his urban and rural environments, industry and nature, innovation and tradition, the past and the future.

On a smaller, more intimate scale, his drawings, watercolors, and especially his pastels more closely approach the Symbolist ideal of *poésie pure*.[83] In these works Stella explores the semiotic potential of certain motifs, abstract forms, and colors to create a visual language that can objectify the subjective. Stella's preoccupation with tree forms, for example, and their centrality to many of his important compositions reveal a strong emotional and physical identification with them, if not directly as self-portraits then as human analogies in the plant world. Beyond the traditional associations of trees and plants with fecundity, growth, and regeneration, Stella often invested his vegetation with erotic overtones that energize their physical forms. In a graphically vivid description of his own sexual awakening, he speaks of "the tree of my young budding life . . . possessed as if by a sudden storm, shook, churned, twisted like a slender tree trunk in March." And in another passage of his notes, he refers to "the trembling trees shaking like virgin limbs quivering with the burning taste of love."[84]

Stella expressed his analogy between the human body and a tree most vividly in drawings of the tropical banyan tree, whose distinctive trunk and limbs readily lend themselves to such a comparison. In several sketches of this tree, the trunks take on distinct characteristics of male and female human

Figure 91

(opposite)
Tree of My Life, 1919
Oil on canvas
83½ x 75½ in.
Mr. and Mrs. Barney A.
Ebsworth Foundation
and Windsor, Inc.

95

torsos (figs. 92, 93). In the first the bulges and knots of the bark resemble breasts and nipples on a graceful, outstretched body, while the heavier, more muscular trunk in the second sketch suggests the sturdier, more masculine forms of upraised arms and powerful tendons. The extent to which Stella emphasized the anthropomorphic characteristics of the natural forms can be seen in the organic, sensual qualities of the outline and the gently modulated surfaces that suggest muscle beneath skin.

In many drawings of trees and plants, Stella focused on the sturdy, intricate root system that anchors and nourishes the tree while its limbs reach for the sky (figs. 94, 95). Drawn carefully and lovingly, roots represent Stella's own strong sense of rootedness, his intense nostalgia for his home-land: "Suddenly we have the sensation that our feet are sinking into the viscera of our mother earth. It reclaims us and repossesses us with maternal jealousy, and we yield ourselves to its warm breath, as when we were small we fell asleep at our mother's breast."[85] An artist with sincere attachment to his own roots, he remained strongly committed to the values and precepts he had learned as a young man and art student, despite his enthusiastic response to many of the formal innovations of the early modernist movements.

Another important motif that recurs throughout his work is the arch form. Gothic arches in particular represented a romantic fascination with the Middle Ages, a period that exemplified for many of Stella's contemporaries a unified, healthy society before rationality and materialism replaced spiritual concerns.[86] Despite Futurism's anti-Gothic ideology, Stella's own fascination with the arch form may include some aspects of this romantic medievalism (see figs. 87, 88). He seems, however, to regard the arch less as a historical form than as an expression of the modern myth of the analogy between the Virgin and the dynamo, the cathedral and the technological wonderwork.[87] Gothic arches represented a technological advance over Romanesque arches, allowing cathedrals to soar higher with less internal support than any previous structures. Arches were also associated with the wonders of modern technology. In his many studies of the Brooklyn Bridge, Stella focused on the Gothic archways as the dominant architectural motif (figs. 96, 97).

Rounded arches had found their way into modern technological wonders, at the base of the Eiffel Tower and in the side bays of the Palace of Machines in Paris, built for the Paris Exposition, 1889–90. Seen from ground level, the arches at the base of the Eiffel Tower dwarf the crowds below like a giant metal rainbow. In fact, the central triangular motif for his *Study for "New York Interpreted"* recalls the shape of the Eiffel Tower, as if Stella

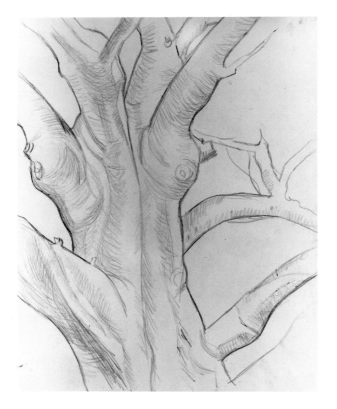

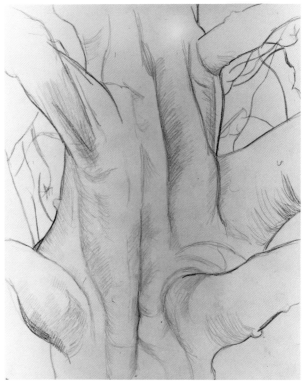

Figure 92

Untitled (Banyan tree),
ca. 1930–39
Pencil
11½ x 9¾ in.
Bernard and Dorothy
Rabin

Figure 93

Untitled (Banyan tree),
ca. 1930–39
Pencil
12 x 9¾ in.
Bernard and Dorothy
Rabin

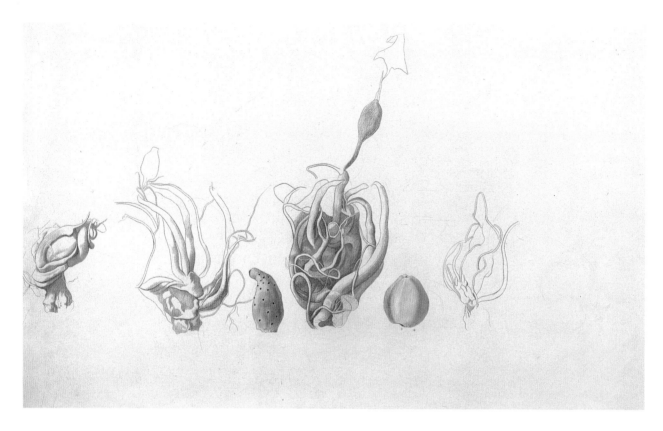

Figure 94

Cactus Roots, ca. 1920–26
Crayon and silverpoint
on prepared paper
21⅞ x 28½ in.
Hirschl and Adler
Galleries, Inc., New
York

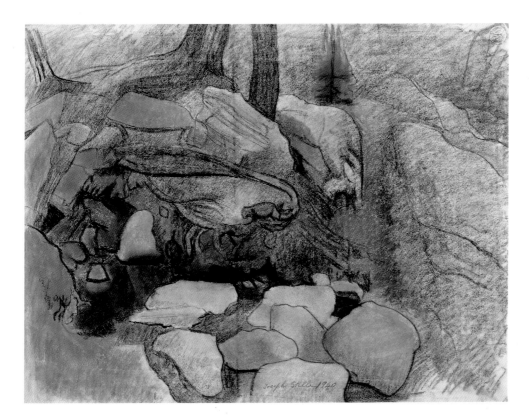

Figure 95

Roots, Bronx Park,
ca. 1940
Pastel
19 x 25¼ in.
Museum of Fine Arts,
Boston, Gift of the Print
and Drawing Club

Figure 96

Brooklyn Bridge,
ca. 1920–22
Charcoal, pastel, and
pencil
40⅜ x 15⅝ in.
Richard York Gallery,
New York

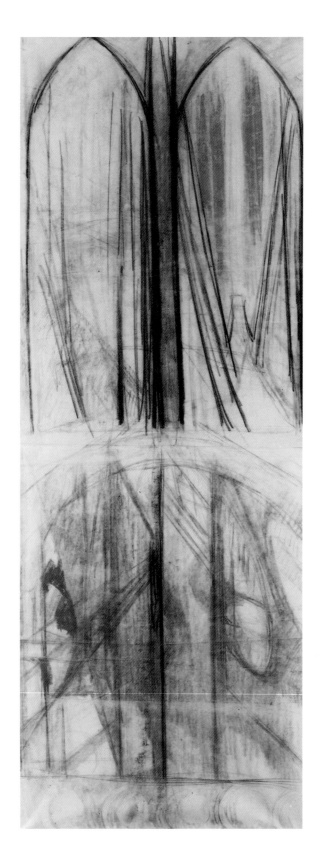

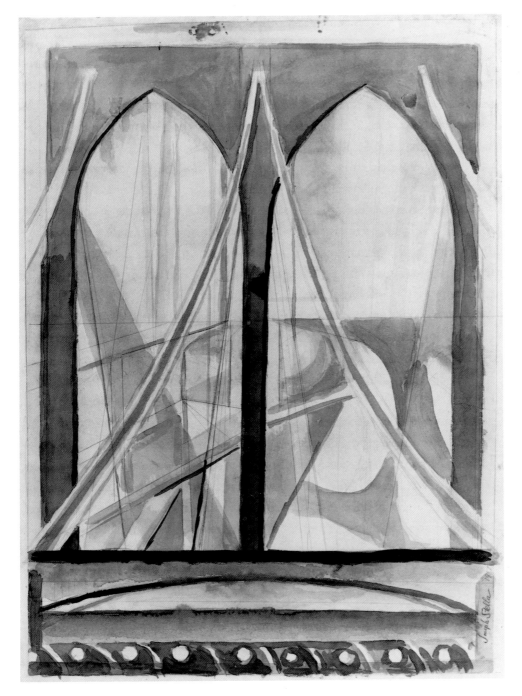

Figure 97

Study for "New York Interpreted," ca. 1917–21
Watercolor
23 x 17 in.
Hirshhorn Museum and
Sculpture Garden,
Smithsonian Institution,
Washington, D.C.,
Gift of the Federal
Bureau of Investigation
(1985.22)

sought to combine the two miracles of modern engineering into a single image.[88] Stella used the arch form simultaneously as a compositional and symbolic device to unify the five sections in his *Study for "New York Interpreted"* (fig. 98). Although he eliminated the arch that spanned all five panels in the final painting, arches appear repeated on a smaller scale throughout the composition as symbolic and decorative elements, much as they recur just above the arches on the Eiffel Tower. Both pointed and rounded arches symbolized the union of modern technology with a sense of spirituality and transcendence that Stella sought to express in his art.

By extending the arch motif to natural forms, such as tree branches, the light effects of a volcanic eruption, or the sound of a bird, Stella expanded the analogy to the eternal qualities of nature (figs. 99, 100; see fig. 90). Tree forms in conjunction with building forms suggest an attempt at a synthesis of urban and rural motifs, natural and artificial forms (see fig. 32). The associations of the arch with rainbows, domes, stained-glass windows, sacred paintings, and church architecture endow natural as well as constructed forms with spiritual overtones (see fig. 88).

The analogy of natural and manufactured forms recurs in the motif of the vertical cylinder. The tall, cylindrical form in the center of *Nocturne* simultaneously alludes to a tree, a telephone pole, and a smokestack or industrial silo (see fig. 57). Describing *The Port*, the first panel of his monumental polyptych *The Voice of the City of New York Interpreted* (see fig. 29), Stella associates the prominent ship's mast and ropes with all these allusions as well: "Against the deep blue-green that dominates the sky and water like a triumphant song of a new religion, there rises the pure cylindrical forms of the smoke stacks . . . the trees of the ship-and-factory forest . . . the black telegraph wires . . . knitting together the far and the near in harmonious unity."[89]

Throughout this monumental work, Stella called on such characteristic Symbolist devices and images as night and a boat at sea, musical analogies, a sense of infinity, and religious allusions to express the complex meaning of his subject:

> I used as time "the night" which invests every element with poetry. I selected as moods of my symphony the PORT, SKY SCRAPERS, THE BRIDGE and THE WHITE WAY. I placed in the center of my composition the SKY SCRAPERS in the form of a prow of a vessel sailing to the infinite, electricity opening at the base as guide with a pair of wings. . . . As a predella to this gigantic steely cathedral I opened the nets of subways and tubes.[90]

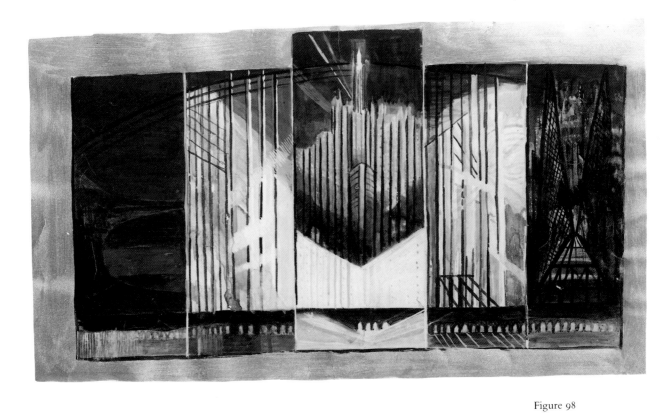

Figure 98

Study for "New York Interpreted,"
ca. 1920
Watercolor and gouache
with metallic border
10¾ x 19¾ in.
Yale University Art
Gallery, New Haven,
Connecticut, Gift from
the estate of Katherine
S. Dreier

Figure 99

Tree and Houses,
ca. 1915–17
Silverpoint and colored
pencil on prepared paper
13¾ x 10⅜
The University of Iowa
Museum of Art, Iowa
City (1983.48)

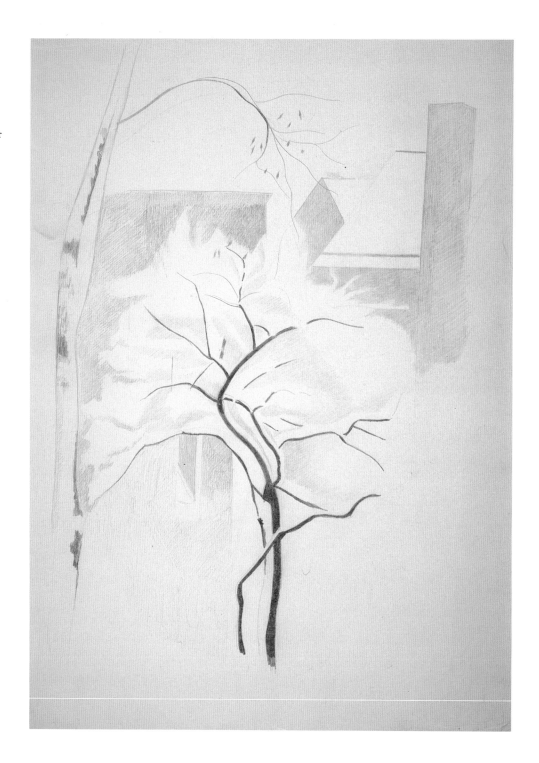

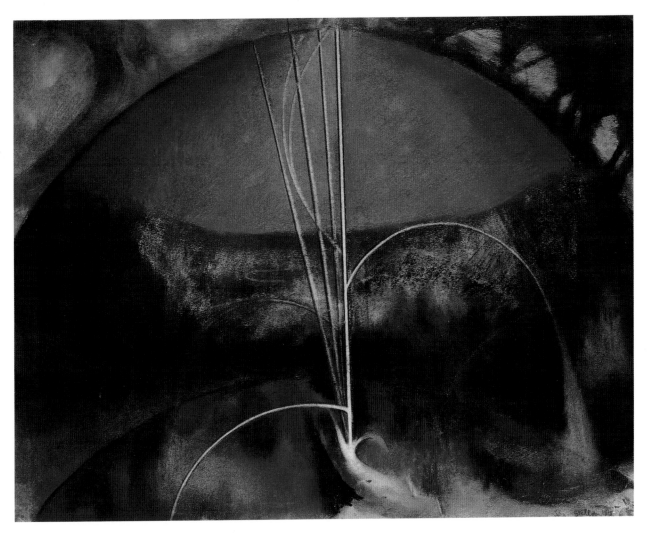

Figure 100

Song of the Nightingale,
ca. 1918
Pastel
18 x 23⅛ in.
Collection, The Museum
of Modern Art,
New York,
Bertram F. and Susie
Brummer Foundation
Fund

Figure 101

Swans, ca. 1924–30
Pastel and charcoal
11¾ in. diameter
Mr. and Mrs. E. D.
Weeks

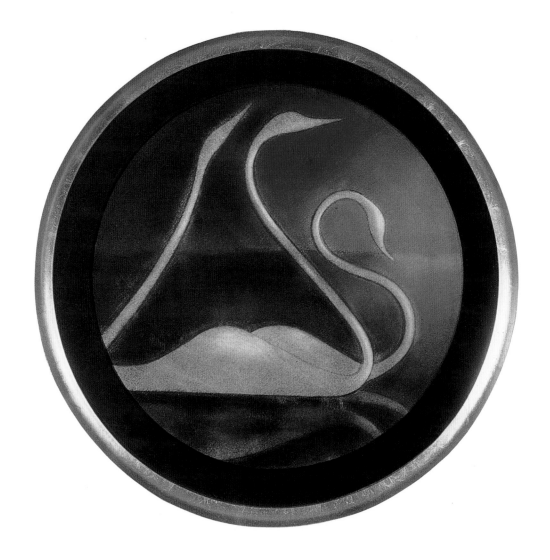

A form that recurs in several of Stella's drawings and paintings is that of a swan, an image favored by the Symbolists not only for its elongated, curvilinear silhouette, but also for the play on words inherent in the French word for swan, *cygne*, and its homonym *signe*, or sign, a sonorous word simultaneously evoking sense and image (fig. 101).[91] Recalling Mallarmé's famous sonnet of the swan, Stella's hallucinatory image in cool colors is a visual equivalent of Symbolist poetry by an artist who sought to unite visual art, music, and poetry into a single expression.

The Transformation of Nature

Color remained a central means of expression for Stella, regardless of the style in which a drawing or painting was executed. In Stella's metalpoint drawings, line itself acquired color—the cool, reflective surface of a silver line or the warm, rich tone of oxidized silver or gold replaces the more neutral character of graphite (fig. 102).[92] Crayons and colored pencils are often used to enhance the subtle colors of his metalpoint lines, giving these works a less descriptive, more sensuous, decorative, or evocative cast (figs. 103, 104).

Arches, cylinders, radiating lines, concentric circles, cloud formations, and other abstract shapes became visual metaphors of Stella's romantic, spiritual aspirations and idealizing visions that infuse both constructed and natural forms with metaphysical dimensions. The radiating forms and dynamic, centrifugal movement in *Abstraction: Mardi Gras* suggest a sunrise as surely as the flamelike petals in *Sunflower* or the central circular motif and radiating palm fronds in *Untitled* (Palm and sun) (figs. 105–7). The brilliantly colored concentric circles in the former might also be seen as halos emanating from a single point of light, a vanishing point suggesting infinity, an invisible and timeless source of creation. The flamelike outline of petals encircling a wide-open eye in *Sunflower* transforms the flower into an image of an all-seeing godhead associated with the sun. The strong central axis of each suggests a hieratic, iconic image. The metallic paint framing *Abstraction: Mardi Gras* further enhances the sense of a precious, even a sacred object.

Stella's nature studies often convey a mood or imply a spiritual dimension by virtue of his presentation. The shading surrounding the "trinity" in *Maple Leaves* enhances its physical presence with a spiritual aura that transcends the material world (fig. 108). Executed in metalpoint on prepared

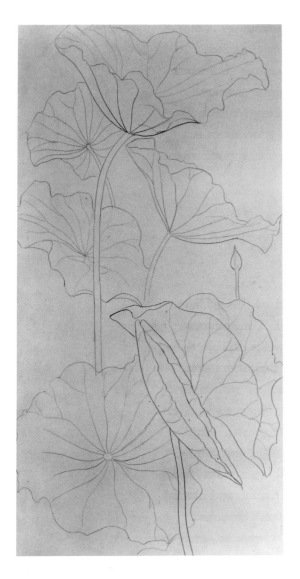

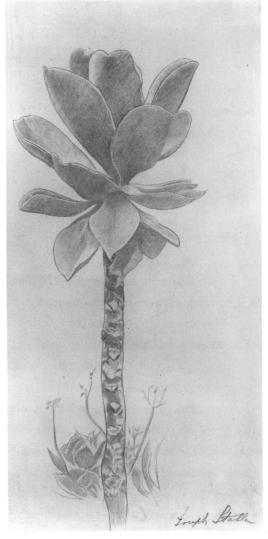

Figure 102

Lotus Leaves
Silverpoint on prepared
paper
14¼ x 7 in.
Karen and Howard B.
Sherman

Figure 103

Flower Study, ca. 1919
Silverpoint and crayon
on prepared paper
12⅞ x 6½ in.
National Museum of
American Art,
Smithsonian Institution,
Washington, D.C.,
Robert Tyler Davis
Memorial Fund

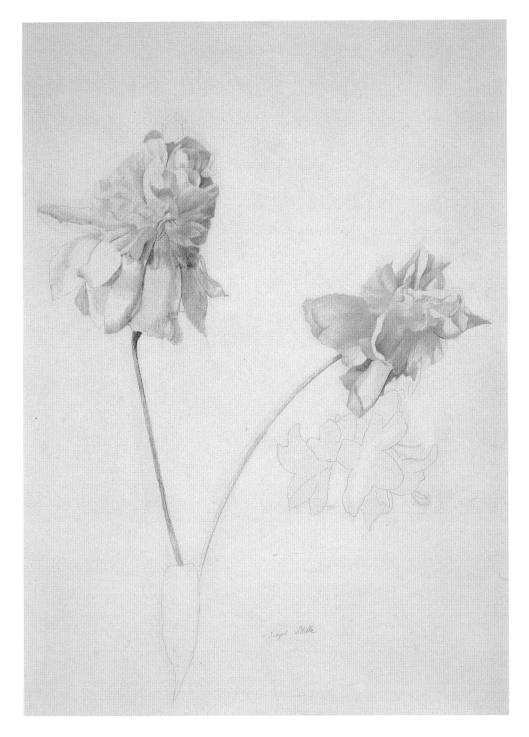

Figure 104

Peonies, ca. 1919
Silverpoint and crayon
on prepared paper
23⅛ x 18½ in.
Amon Carter Museum,
Fort Worth

109

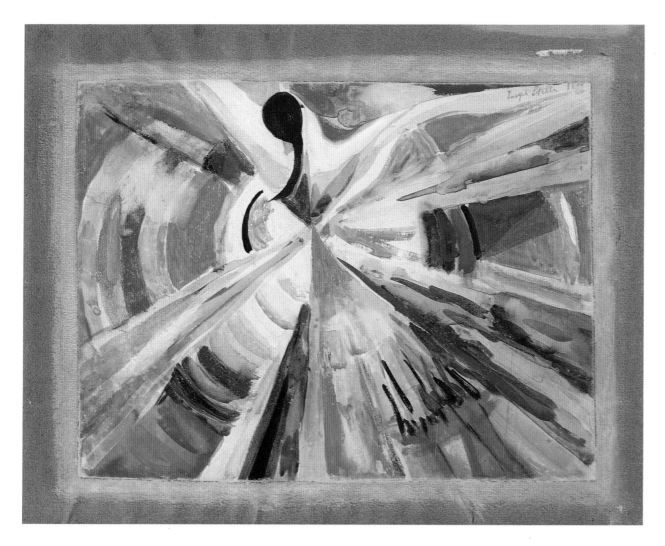

Figure 105

Abstraction: Mardi Gras,
ca. 1914–16
Watercolor, gouache,
pencil, and metallic paint
on colored paper
11⅛ x 13¹²⁄₁₆ in. (approx.)
Hirshhorn Museum and
Sculpture Garden,
Smithsonian Institution,
Washington, D.C., The
Joseph H. Hirshhorn
Bequest

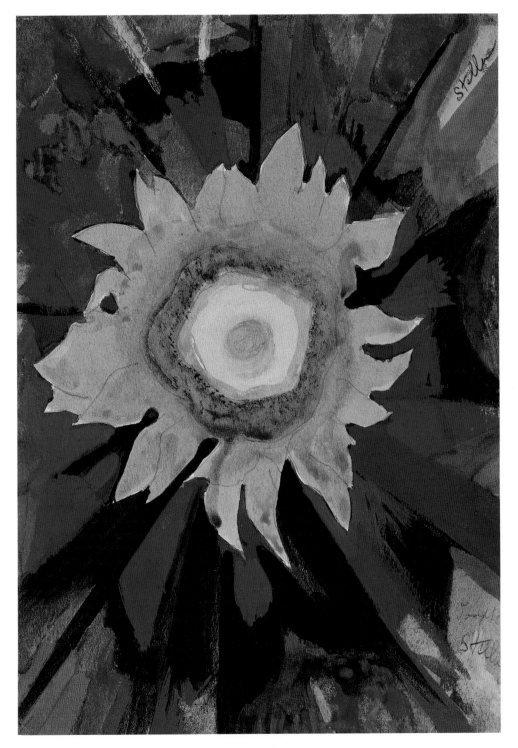

Figure 106

Sunflower
Pencil, gouache,
tempera, and varnish
9¼ x 6⅜ in.
Mr. and Mrs. Maurice
Katz

Figure 107

Untitled (Palm and sun)
Watercolor and gouache
11⅞ x 8⅞ in.
Bernard and Dorothy
Rabin

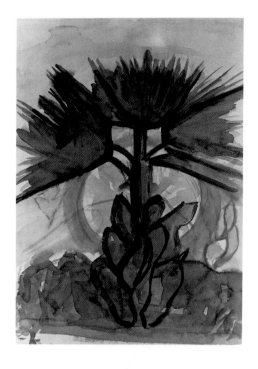

Figure 108

Maple Leaves, ca. 1910
Metalpoint on prepared
paper
9¹¹⁄₁₆ x 6¹⁵⁄₁₆ in.
The Ackland Art
Museum, The University
of North Carolina at
Chapel Hill, Ackland
Fund

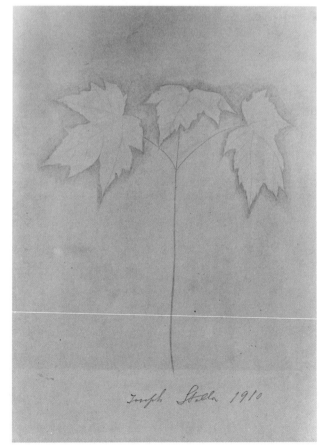

paper, the warm, golden, reflective line invests the form with transcendental intensity. The rich colors and heavy outlines of the iconically frontal croton plant, enthroned majestically in front of an archlike araceous leaf, acquire an almost religious solemnity in the presence of a dark, rectangular backdrop (fig. 109).[93]

The gracefully animated tendrils of the statuesque *Lupine* composition wave Shivalike as if to embrace the more suppliant flowering stem that gently brushes the taller, more erect plant (fig. 110). Unlike the more delicate, ethereal expressions of most of his flower drawings, overtones of passion, lust, and death are manifest in the dangerously poisonous amaryllis depicted in *Study for "The Red Flower,"* brilliantly red and outlined in bold black, with pollen heavy on the stamen tips (fig. 111). The dynamic vigor and virility of youth are suggested by the sharply erect stalks and delicate, coral-red blossoms of the Skyrocket plant, variously known as Red Hot Poker, Flame Flower, Torch Lily, or Triton's Spear, shown close-up on a sweeping diagonal in the fullness of its life cycle before the stalk begins to droop and the petals change to orange and then greenish-yellow (fig. 112).

Sensuality and spirituality were intimately linked in Stella's depictions of flowers, more closely akin to Hinduism than to the Christian dichotomy of body and spirit. The curvilinear rhythms in *Lotus Bud* (fig. 113) or *Lotus Leaves* (see fig. 102) suggest internal animation or invisible energy.[94] The act of drawing itself became a sensuous experience: "I was seized with a sensual thrill in cutting with the sharpness of my silverpoint the terse purity of the lotus leaves or the matchless stem of a strange tropical plant."[95] In a later version of this subject (fig. 114), his freer and more expressionistic handling of line and color suggests the passion and sensuality he continued to associate with this flower.

To what extent Stella was aware of the symbolic meanings of specific flowers can only be a matter of speculation, but his continuing fascination with lotus buds and waterlilies suggests at least some familiarity with the rich lore and meanings associated with this flower in many civilizations over thousands of years. A symbol of the sun, fertility, immortality, eternal youth, resurrection, paradise, perfection, purity, and beauty, this plant embodied the sort of universal symbolism that appealed to Stella's visionary romanticism.

What distinguishes Stella's treatment of natural form from descriptive naturalism is the vitality with which he endows his subjects, his selectivity of detail, and the major role his imagination plays in his juxtapositions and

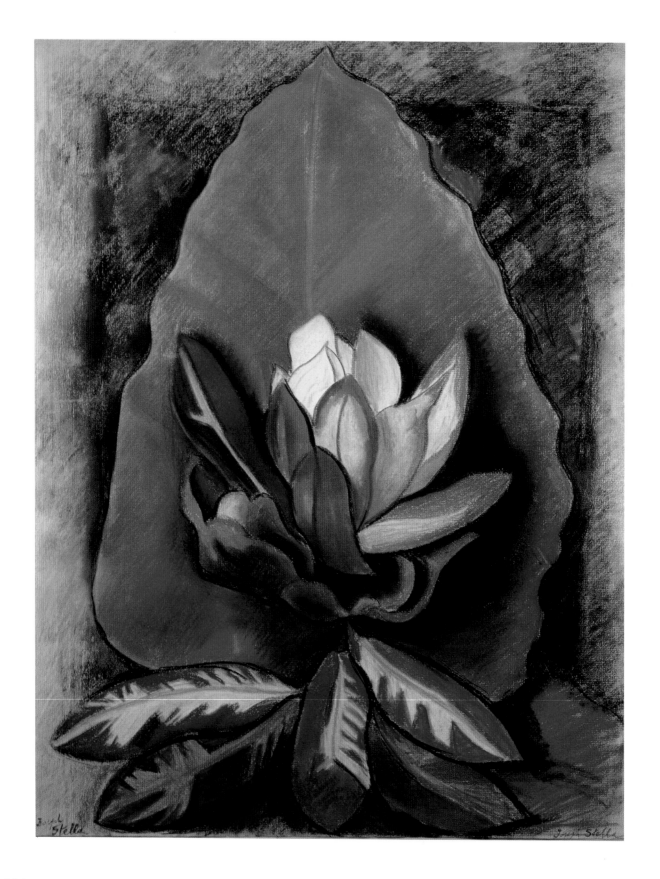

114

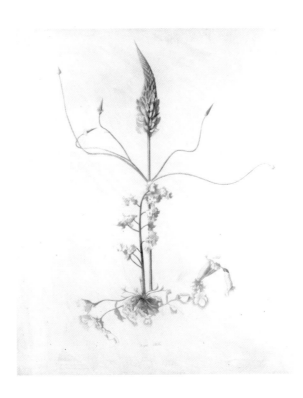

Figure 109

(opposite)

*Flower Study with Croton
Leaves*, ca. 1940
Pastel
25 x 18¾ in.
Drs. Sheldon and
Lillibeth Boruchow

Figure 110

Lupine, ca. 1919
Silverpoint and crayon
on prepared paper
27½ x 21½ in.
Collection of Tobin
Surveys

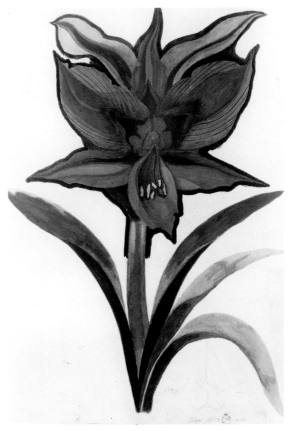

Figure 111

*Study for "The Red
Flower"*
Watercolor and gouache
31 x 22 in.
Private collection

Figure 112

Tropical Flowers
Watercolor with casein
25 x 18 in.
Mr. and Mrs. Carl D.
Lobell

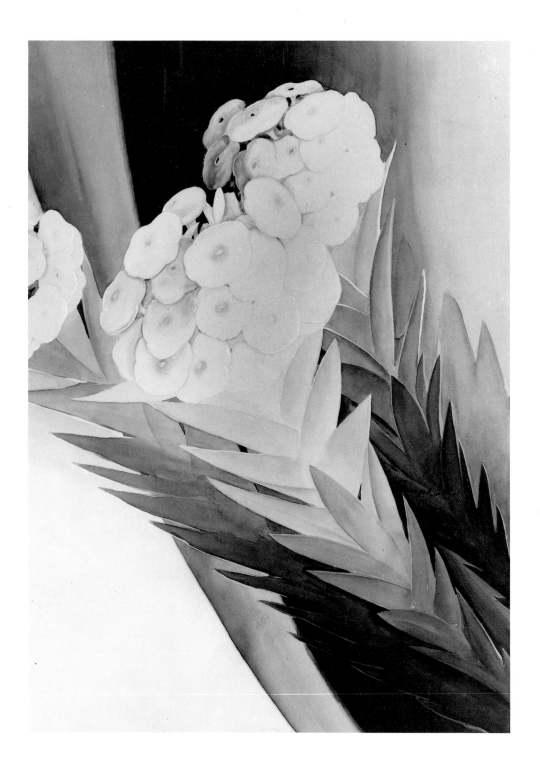

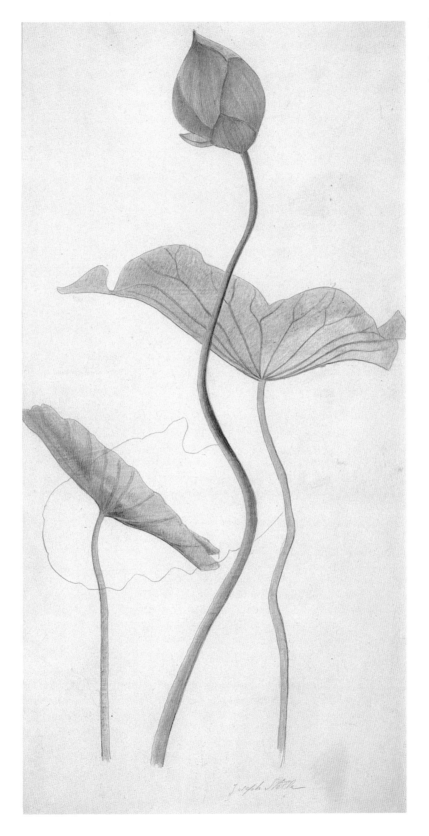

Figure 113

Lotus Bud, ca. 1920–26
Metalpoint and crayon
14¾ x 7⅛ in.
Mr. and Mrs. Carl
Freeman

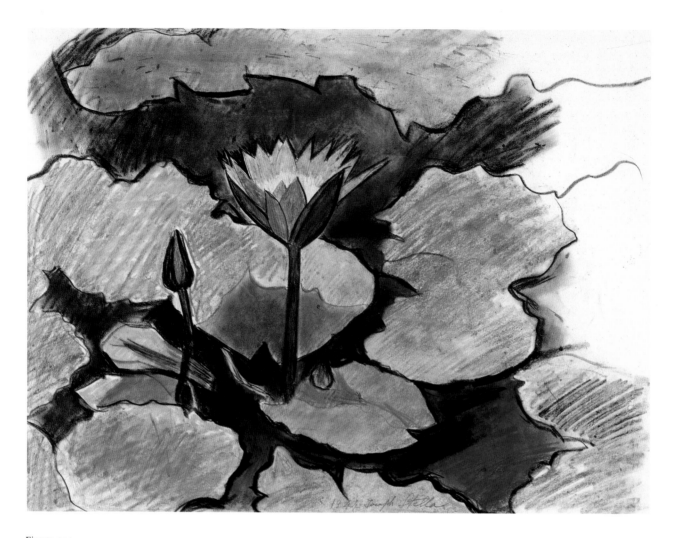

Figure 114

Purple Waterlilies, 1944
Charcoal and pastel
17½ x 23⅜ in.
Private collection

compositions of flowers. Imaginative combinations of flora, as in *Cactus and Tropical Foliage* or *Flower and Butterfly*, reveal the extent to which Stella took poetic license in rearranging nature (figs. 115, 116). The very intensity of his focus and clarity of his line transform the images into visual abstractions as surely as does the bold simplification of form in *Tree Study* (fig. 117) or *Tree and Houses* (see fig. 99). The attenuated linear elegance of *Slender Green Stalk*, describing a form that cannot be identified as a specific botanical specimen, seems to defy gravity and materiality (fig. 118).[96]

Exquisite drawings of flowers, birds, and trees make up a large and important segment of Stella's work on paper. His antirealist, antiscientific bias did not preclude a careful study of nature's forms. Although such carefully observed and minutely rendered studies as *Flower Study* or *Peonies* (see figs. 103, 104) suggest almost scientific accuracy and illusionistic veracity, their delicacy and gracefulness convey an otherworldly perfection that transports the plants from the material world into the realm of the ideal, as "flowers symbolic of the daring flights of our spiritual life."[97] In his exquisite study *Still Life with Plums*, the delicately rendered fruits seem to float weightless in space in the center of the sheet, held together in timeless suspension by the tension generated between the horizontal and vertical forms (fig. 119).

The complex relationship between abstraction, symbolism, and representation in Stella's most successful work suggests multiple levels of private meaning and allusion that reverberate throughout his drawings and paintings. He was fond of repeating an incident from his childhood, recounted as a parable to illustrate his love of freedom:

> I was eight years old and my hatred for the school was assuming alarming proportions . . . in a glorious day of May the window was open and I was looking at the blossoms of a cherry tree in full bloom. A bird came. I thought he was saying "Come and have fun outside." As pushed by the imperative force of fate I rushed straight to the teacher.
>
> "I have to go out."
> "Why?"
> "He is calling me."
> "Who?"
> "The bird."[98]

Even in his most literal reference to this story, the exquisite delicacy of the form, graceful, curvilinear movement and rhythms, and ethereal, blue aura in

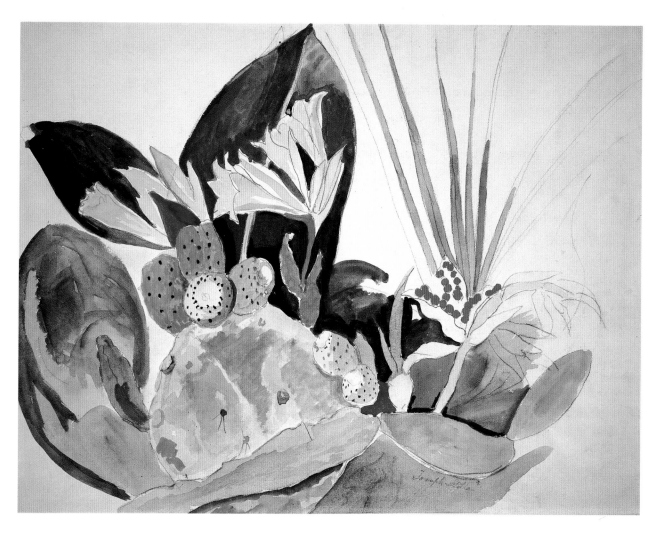

Figure 115

Cactus and Tropical
Foliage
Watercolor over graphite
18⅛ x 24⅛ in.
Museum of Fine Arts,
Boston, Sophie M.
Friedman Fund

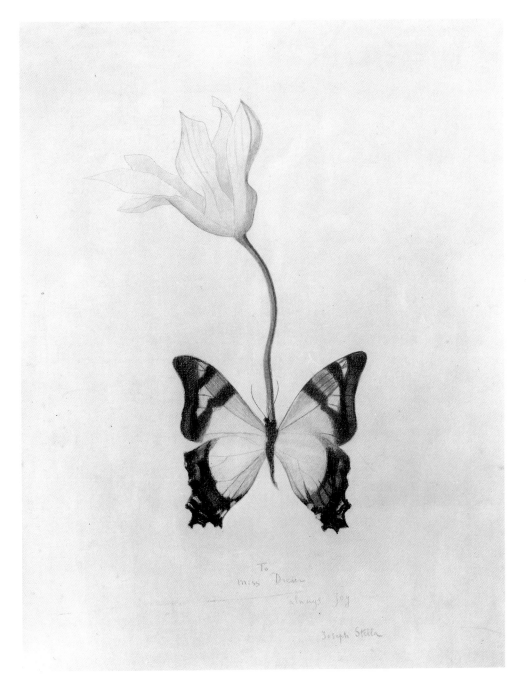

Figure 116

Flower and Butterfly, ca. 1922
Metalpoint and crayon on prepared paper
14⅛ x 11⅛ in.
Yale University Art Gallery, New Haven, Connecticut, From the estate of Katherine S. Dreier

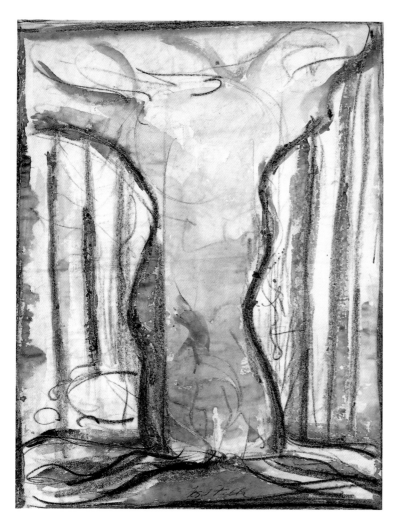

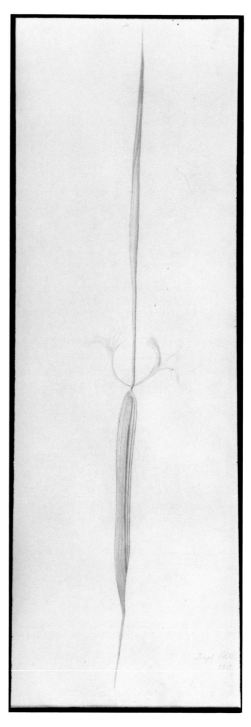

Figure 117

Tree Study
Crayon and wash
20 x 15½ in.
Bernard and Dorothy
Rabin

Figure 118

Slender Green Stalk, ca. 1919
Silverpoint and crayon
21 x 7 in.
Jordan-Volpe Gallery,
Inc., New York

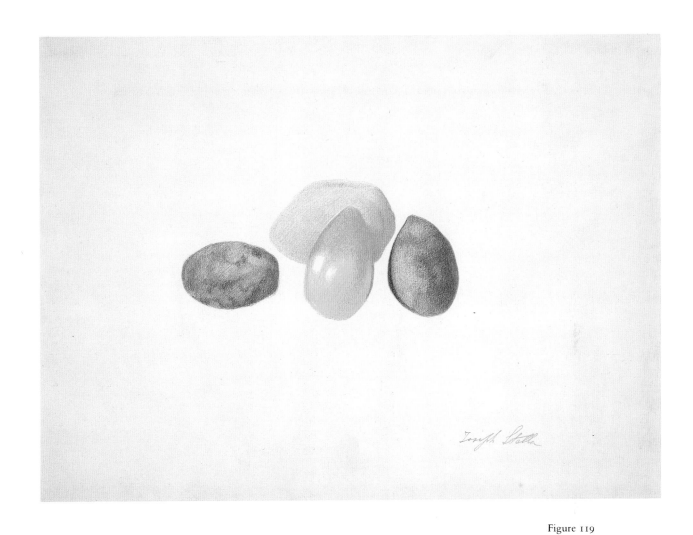

Figure 119

Still Life with Plums,
ca. 1920–26
Metalpoint and colored
pencil on prepared paper
11 x 14 in.
Museum of Fine Arts,
Boston, Sophie M.
Friedman Fund

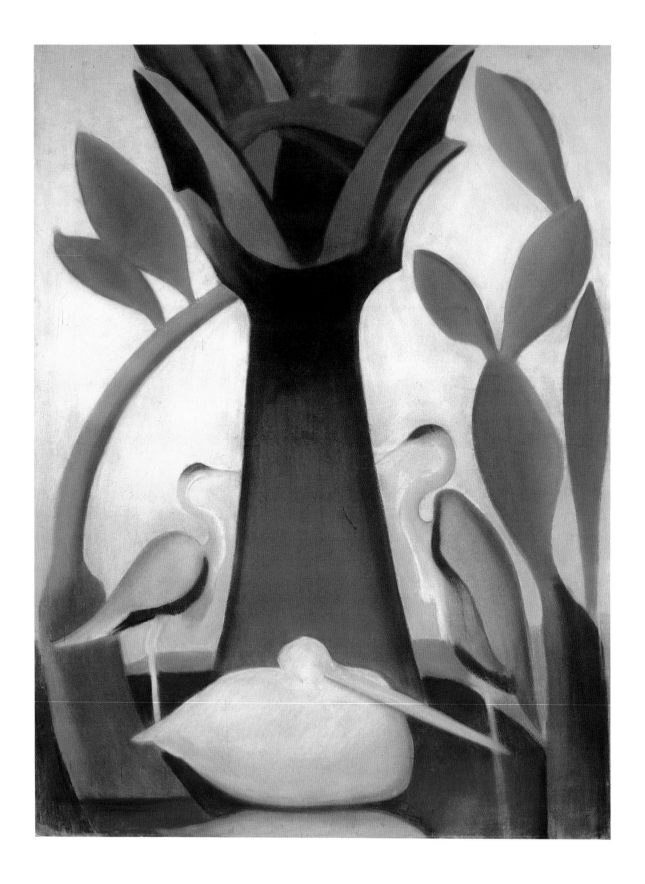

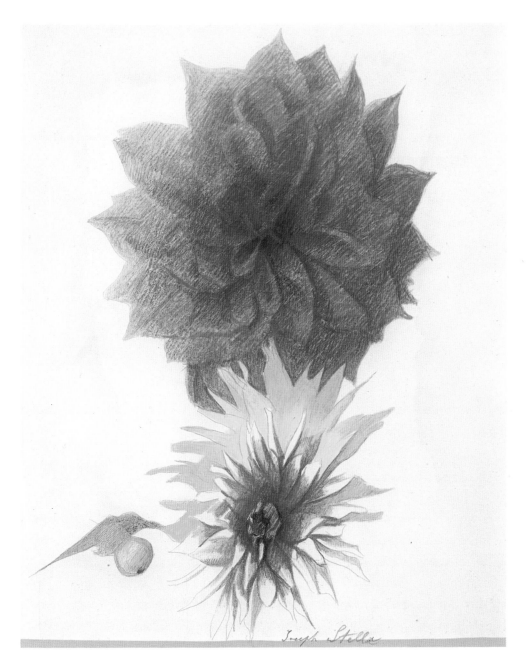

Figure 120

(opposite)
The Palm (Herons),
ca. 1926
Pastel on paperboard
43½ x 32⅝ in.
Hirshhorn Museum and
Sculpture Garden,
Smithsonian Institution,
Washington, D.C., Gift
of Joseph H. Hirshhorn,
1966

Figure 121

Dahlias
Silverpoint and crayon
on prepared paper
11⅛ x 9 in.
Dr. and Mrs. Harold
Rifkin

the background transport the image from the representation of nature to the realm of myth (see figs. 26, 27). Similarly, the strongly hieratic composition of *The Palm (Herons)* suggests a timeless, idealized, if enigmatic world in which natural forms assume abstract significance by virtue of their simplification, symmetrical placement, and monumental scale (fig. 120).

As a young boy Stella believed that the song of birds had a spiritual meaning unknown to all except poets, mystics, and saints.[99] A recurring theme in his drawings, a bird or birds near a flower or tree became for Stella a personal symbol of his independence from artistic movements and academic proscriptions, of rebellion, escape, flight, music, and recognition of a spiritual force far greater than his own will (fig. 121): "The first need of the artist is absolute freedom—freedom from schools, from critics, advisors and the so called friends. The Artist that will please himself will please others. . . . Birds sing to pour out their joy of living."[100]

Music for the Eye

The complexity of Stella's allusions is perhaps best illustrated by one of his most thoroughly abstract works, *Song of the Nightingale* (see fig. 100).[101] On a narrative level, one assumes that the light-colored form at the bottom center of the composition represents the nightingale, while the radiating and curved lines, resembling a musical scale, depict a visualization of its song. The central motif seems to have been based directly on a composition by Francis Picabia, *La musique est comme la peinture* (Music Is Like Painting) (ca. 1913–17; N. Manoukian Collection). This painting was first documented in New York at the 1917 exhibition of the Society of Independent Artists, with which Stella was closely involved, and the reference would have been apparent to other artists in Stella's circle of friends. The lines in Picabia's painting are based directly on a diagram of the effect of a magnetic field on alpha, beta, and gamma particles and represent an attempt to make visible the invisible. This concept is further reinforced in the titles of Stella's and Picabia's works, both of which refer to music. Picabia's title, *Music Is Like Painting*, clearly asserts the Symbolist concept of correspondence, to which Stella, in *Song of the Nightingale,* seems to respond: "Painting is like music."

References to music abound in his titles and writings. Stella's many nocturnes and several versions of *Song of the Birds, Der Rosenkavalier, Tropical Sonata, Serenade, Neapolitan Song,* and *Song of Barbados* are among his most important works. References to music appear so frequently in his writings that even works without specific mention of musical themes in their titles were apparently conceived as music-inspired compositions. The most prominent example is *New York Interpreted,* which he envisioned as a symphony in five movements (i.e., panels), with an elaborate rhythmic and harmonic structure based on line and color.[102]

The pervasiveness of musical references in Stella's work recalls his early admiration for Whistler, who declared: "As music is the poetry of sound, so is painting the poetry of sight" and who titled many of his paintings Nocturnes, Arrangements, Symphonies, and Harmonies.[103] Concurrently, the concept of "color music" developed into a visionary new art form as an outgrowth of the Romantic and Symbolist movements. Related to the concepts of musical analogy and color music was the notion of synesthesia, a quasi-mystical and pseudoscientific belief in the subjective interaction of all sensory perceptions.[104]

The exact source of Stella's adoption of musical analogy is unclear. It is more likely that his sources were many, among them Whistler, Kandinsky, Picabia, or perhaps even his American contemporaries, Stieglitz, Hartley, Weber, Dove, and O'Keeffe, for whom musical analogy and synesthesia were significant aesthetic elements. What does seem evident, however, is the strength of Stella's commitment to these ideas and their critical importance as the source of his own approach to abstraction. Through color analogy and synesthesia, Stella could address the formal elements of his work—color, line, composition—and simultaneously evoke sensual pleasure, emotional fervor, symbolic meaning, and spiritual intensity.

Stella's inclination toward musical analogy and receptivity to theories of color music and synesthesia were shared by other artists of his generation. Many subscribed to Emerson's doctrine of the universality of artistic expression, which encouraged experimentation in various forms of expression and closer bonds between painters, writers, musicians, dancers, and dramatists, regarding the arts as one, united in a universal spirit of mind and divided only in medium. Emerson's ideas and idealistic hopes for American civilization were transmitted to young artists of the early twentieth century through the works and personality of Whitman, whose optimism and enthusiasm captured their imagination.

A Window into the Mind

The highly personal, subjective quality of Stella's imagery is nowhere more apparent than in the visual puns and erotic overtones that characterize some of his drawings, revealing a sense of humor that rarely shows through in his paintings. The blossom in *Bird of Paradise and Cactii* seems to alight like an abstract bird on a stem that penetrates the space between two succulent, yet prickly plant forms suggestive of female genitalia (fig. 122).[105] The overt sensuality and whimsical juxtapositions in many of his drawings from nature inject a note of fantasy that is sometimes more amusing than sensual (fig. 123).

One of Stella's most intriguing compositions is a pastel underwater fantasy with darting fish and luxuriant foliage (fig. 124). The plants are however, spiky succulents and cacti, more typical of a desert environment, and the fish are hardly distinguishable from the plant forms. With its ambiguity and analogy, this enigmatic marriage of opposites is strongly reminiscent of Symbolist submarine fantasy visions. Mysterious and disorienting, the graceful curvilinear forms and brilliant colors illumined by an intense white light from above suggest a mystical phenomenon entirely removed from rational experience.

The goldfish theme recalls a series of paintings by Matisse done in the spring of 1912, just after he returned to Paris from Morocco. This contact with Matisse may also have been the source of his fascination with North Africa and the impetus for his later trip to Biskra in Algeria, where Matisse had visited in 1906, at a time when Matisse too had been seeking to express a spiritual force in his art unrelated to religious dogma (see fig. 25).[106] Although goldfish images were common in Paris exhibitions in 1911–12, reflecting an interest in oriental motifs, their juxtaposition with desert vegetation recalls Matisse's association of them with Morocco, where they were objects of contemplation.[107]

The prominence of the gold and silver fish suggests that a pun may have been intended on *poisson*, the French word for fish, and the name of the French alchemist Albert Poisson, whose inexpensive paperback publication, *Théories et symboles des alchimistes* (1891), may have been the source of the references to the occult in Duchamp's work during the time when Stella was Duchamp's friend.[108] Cryptography was a popular topic of discussion at the evening gatherings at the Arensberg apartment, and puns were particularly favored by Duchamp and Man Ray, with whom Stella had a close association

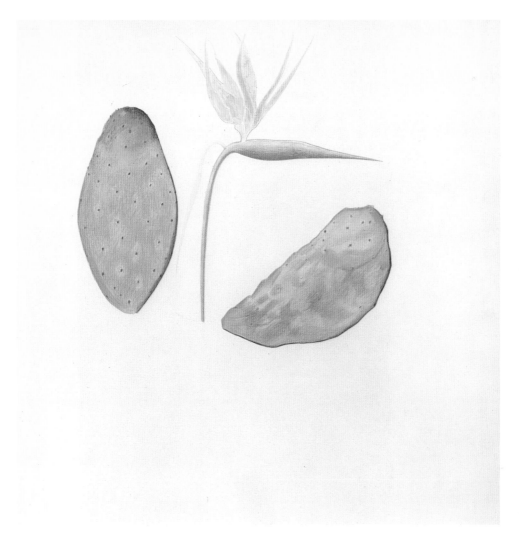

Figure 122

Bird of Paradise and Cactii,
ca. 1920–26
Metalpoint and colored
pencil on prepared paper
28½ x 22½ in.
Hirschl and Adler
Galleries, Inc.,
New York

Figure 123

Still Life, ca. 1939
Pastel
28³⁄₁₆ x 21⁵⁄₈ in.
Hirshhorn Museum and
Sculpture Garden,
Smithsonian Institution,
Washington, D.C., Gift
of Joseph H. Hirshhorn,
1966

Figure 124

(opposite)
Goldfish, ca. 1919–22
Pastel
30 x 23³⁄₈ in.
Watkins Collection,
American University,
Washington, D.C.

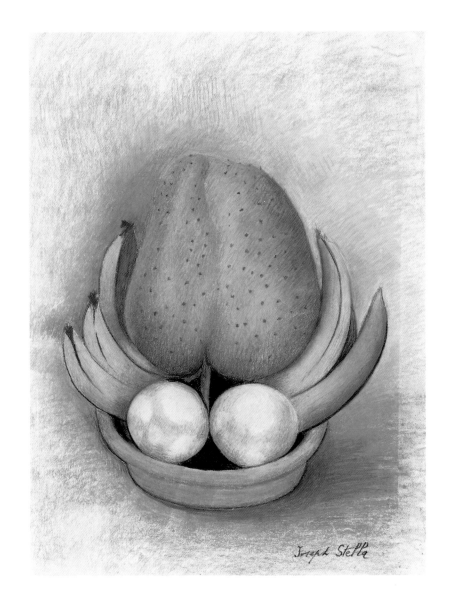

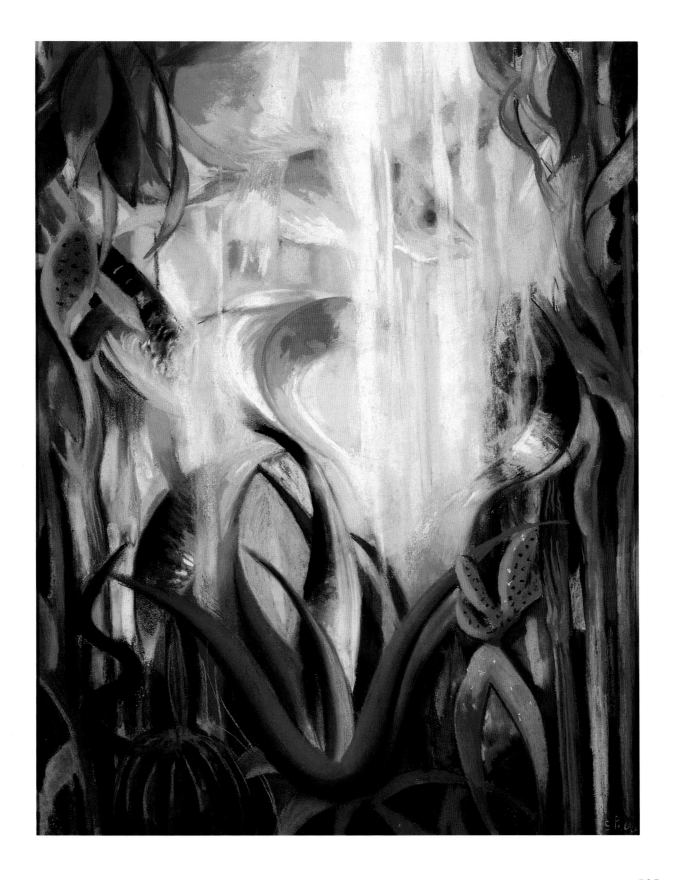

through their mutual involvement with the Arensberg circle, the Society of Independent Artists exhibition of 1917, and the Société Anonyme.[109]

The art movement with which the Arensberg circle was most closely associated was Dada, or more specifically a New York version of the disparate European movement centered in Paris, Zurich, Berlin, and Cologne. Duchamp, Man Ray, and Picabia were the ringleaders of the New York Dada group, and their activities and ideas became a focal point for the diverse interests represented in the Arensberg circle. The Dada spirit continued to be felt in the early years of the Société Anonyme, an organization initiated in 1920 by Duchamp and Man Ray at the instigation of Katherine Dreier, to serve as a forum for the exhibition and promotion of the most avant-garde ideas in contemporary art.

Despite Stella's close association with Duchamp and Man Ray,[110] his involvement in many of the escapades of the New York Dada group, participation in the exhibitions and lectures sponsored by the Société Anonyme, and inclusion in the *Salon Dada, Exposition Internationale* at the Galerie Montaigne in Paris in June 1922, his commitment to Dada principles was tenuous at best. As he had done with Futurism, Stella seems to have adopted only those ideas that were meaningful to him, while ignoring the more radical implications of the movement. Although Stella's friendship with Duchamp was very important at a key moment in his artistic development, the life-affirming optimism of Whitman, stimulating possibilities of modern art, and tenacious hold of artistic tradition kept Stella from embracing the more negative, iconoclastic aspects of Dada beliefs. "Dada means having a good time—the theatre, the dance, the dinner. . . . It is a movement that does away with everything that has always been taken seriously. To poke fun at, to break down, to laugh at, that is Dadaism," he proclaimed after his lecture on modern art in 1921 at the Société Anonyme.[111] An artist who believed that "art was always my only reason of existence, everything was centered and focused on her, and no hardship or difficulties of any sort with events and human beings, would have the power of extinguishing this sacred fire always burning into me,"[112] Stella did not accept the anti-art implications of Dada. Although he relished the intellectual license to break the rules, flaunt tradition, challenge middle-class standards, and question the nature of art, he was not prepared to renounce the past completely or deny the intrinsic value of art.

On the contrary, Stella's relationship with Duchamp and his flirtation with Dada were the catalysts for some of his most extraordinary work. His glass paintings of the late teens and early 1920s appear to have been directly influenced by Duchamp's *Large Glass* (1915–23; Philadelphia Museum of Art), especially his *Man in an Elevated (Train)* (1918; Washington University Gallery of Art, St. Louis).[113] Substituting his own self-portrait for Duchamp's anonymous bachelor machine, Stella affirms his strong identification with Duchamp and the bachelorlike lives they led during the years of their friendship. Reinforcing the allusion to celibacy is the priestlike white collar and dark jacket. In the collage that appears to be a study for this work (fig. 125), the converging lines beneath the broad-brimmed hat recall the single-point perspective so rigorously adhered to in the mechanical "bachelor" section of the *Large Glass*. A Cubist drawing with transparent, interpenetrating planes and abstracted forms, the collaged newspaper fragments, representing an actual newspaper, refer to a technical or scientific subject in the text and ironically to the " 'Lilliputian Bazaar' Baby Book" in the headlines.

In addition to the conceptual and personal references to Duchamp's *Large Glass* in this collage and glass painting, the subject and composition recall a group of analytical studies of a head against a light and a window frame by the Futurist Umberto Boccioni.[114] Painting on glass recalls Kandinsky's and Hartley's works in this medium around this time as well as the decorative brilliance of stained-glass windows. The multilayered references and meanings, symbolic content, and modernist formal devices in Stella's collage and glass painting reveal an artist attempting to synthesize a broad spectrum of ideas into a richly reverberating personal expression.

A Modernist on His Own Terms

Stella's strong sense of independence and ardent belief in freedom of artistic expression kept him from becoming too intimately involved with any one group or art movement. Instead, he had friends and acquaintances among several different groups. Never part of the Stieglitz circle of artists, he nonetheless shared many of their values and interests. Like Stella, Hartley and O'Keeffe studied with William Merritt Chase very early in their careers.[115] The close visual relationship of Stella's tonal landscape drawings for *The Survey* magazine to the pictorialist aesthetic of the photographs of Steichen and Stieglitz has already been noted. His tendency toward a spiritualized, Symbolist interpretation of his subject closely parallels such interests on the part of Dove, Hartley, and O'Keeffe.[116]

Figure 125

Man Reading a Newspaper, 1918
Collage of pencil,
charcoal, and newspaper
15 x 15½ in.
Gertrude Stein Gallery,
New York

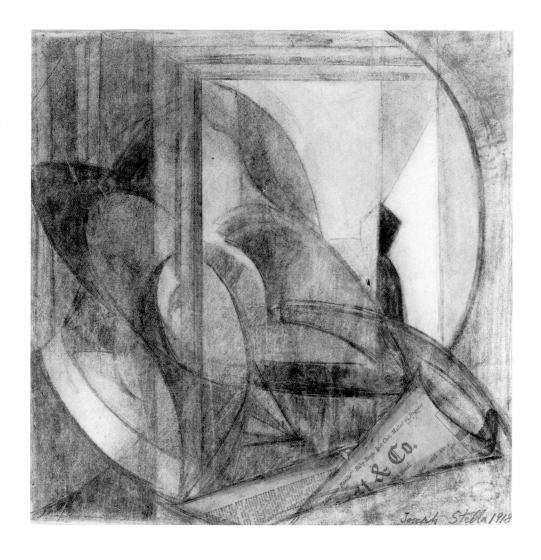

Although Stella's admiration for Whitman seems to have predated his arrival in the United States, the blossoming esteem of the Stieglitz circle for Whitman during and after World War I was another important area of mutual interest. He also shared with the artists of the Stieglitz circle a strong belief in synesthesia as well as an avid admiration for European modernism and an internationalist perspective at odds with the strong nationalist and isolationist sentiments prevalent in the United States before World War I. Like these artists, Stella embraced the stylistic innovations of modernism. Still, Stella maintained his independence from this group, even though he had contact with some of the individual artists, especially with those who were also part of the Arensberg circle.[117]

The Stieglitz group included writers, painters, photographers, political activists, and intellectuals, while the Arensberg circle was made up of writers, musicians, and poets as well as artists. John Marin, Max Weber, Hartley, and Stella wrote extensively, while Sherwood Anderson and Hart Crane painted as well as wrote. One of Stella's closest friends in the Arensberg circle was the French-born composer Edgard Varèse (see fig. 19), who, like Stella, served on the executive board of the International Composers' Guild in the early 1920s.[118] Stella sang with a soft, sweet tenor voice and recited from memory long passages of poetry and excerpts from Shakespeare. In 1923 he designed the "décor" for a performance entitled *L'arbre de ma vie* performed by the actress-singer Georgette Leblanc at her theater in Greenwich Village.[119]

Stella was much more directly involved with the artists, writers, and musicians who frequented the New York apartment of Louise and Walter Arensberg on West Sixty-seventh Street.[120] In contrast to the Stieglitz group, the Arensberg salon was more international in character and included people with a greater diversity of interests and backgrounds. Unlike the autocratic Stieglitz, Arensberg was more receptive to the ideas of other people, and his own interests in symbolism and poetry, especially in Dante, closely paralleled those of Stella.

When the Arensbergs abruptly left for California in 1921, Stella increased his involvement with the Société Anonyme, through which he continued to have access to the latest European art. With the departure of Duchamp and Man Ray for Paris, also in 1921, the influence of Dada in the Société Anonyme waned, and Katherine Dreier's own interests and philosophy came to dominate the organization's activities. Dreier remained very supportive of Stella's work over the years. She purchased several of his most important paintings for the collection of the Société Anonyme, including *Brooklyn Bridge* (see fig. 28), and exhibited his monumental polyptych *The Voice of the City of New York Interpreted* (see fig. 29) in 1923, soon after it was completed. She acquired several of his drawings for her personal collection as well[121] and remained a friend throughout his career. Beyond his gratitude for her personal support, Stella shared with Dreier a strong interest in spiritual concerns, which she expressed through an ardent fascination with Theosophy and wholehearted admiration for the work of Kandinsky. In the face of strong political isolationism and a growing sense of nationalism among American artists, Stella and Dreier were among a diminishing number of supporters of an internationalist perspective. Although Stella lectured and exhibited with the Société Anonyme in the early 1920s, his affiliation with the organization gradually weakened until all that remained was an infrequent correspondence with Dreier.

Succumbing to the intense nostalgia for Italy he had expressed in *Tree of My Life*, he visited Naples, Pompeii, Herculaneum, Paestum, and Capri in 1922, returning to New York in time for the opening of his exhibition at the Société Anonyme in January 1923. For the better part of the years from 1926 to 1935, Stella lived in Paris, making several trips to Italy (fig. 126) and North Africa (see fig. 25). In 1937 he made a stimulating and productive trip to Barbados (fig. 127), and in 1938 returned to Paris and Italy one last time (see fig. 7). Although he continued to paint, his itinerant lifestyle was much more conducive to working on paper. Exhibiting regularly in both the United States and Europe, Stella never again painted on the grand scale of *New York Interpreted.*

The imagery in his drawings, however, became more monumentally scaled, filling the sheet more completely than in similar compositions of an earlier date. The looser, more expressionistic handling of *Three Miners* (fig. 128), in contrast to the more descriptive rendering of *In the Bread Line at Wood's Run* (see fig. 44) or the more dramatic composition *Miners* (see fig. 51), conveys a level of emotional intensity missing from the earlier versions of this subject. His profile portrait of Clara Fasano, his portrait of a peasant from Muro Lucano (see fig. 7), or his still-life composition *Red Pepper* reveal a boldness and assurance in his drawings that had become less pronounced in his later paintings (figs. 129, 130). Even in his depiction of such intimate subjects as a sketch of Clara Fasano sleeping, the large scale and the close-up perspective transform the image from an incidental sketch to a compelling design of subtly varied line and delicate color patterns (see fig. 41). Similarly, the simplicity of his composition for *Path in Barbados*, a stately procession of

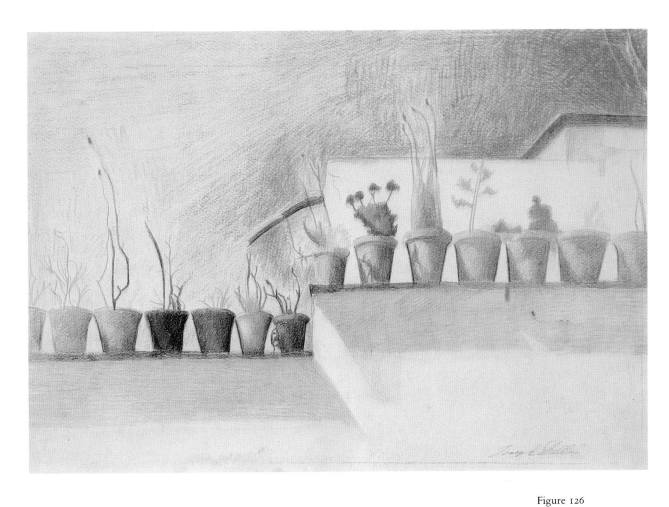

Figure 126

Canzone Napoletana,
ca. 1928
Pencil and crayon
11½ x 16¾ in. (irregular)
Private collection

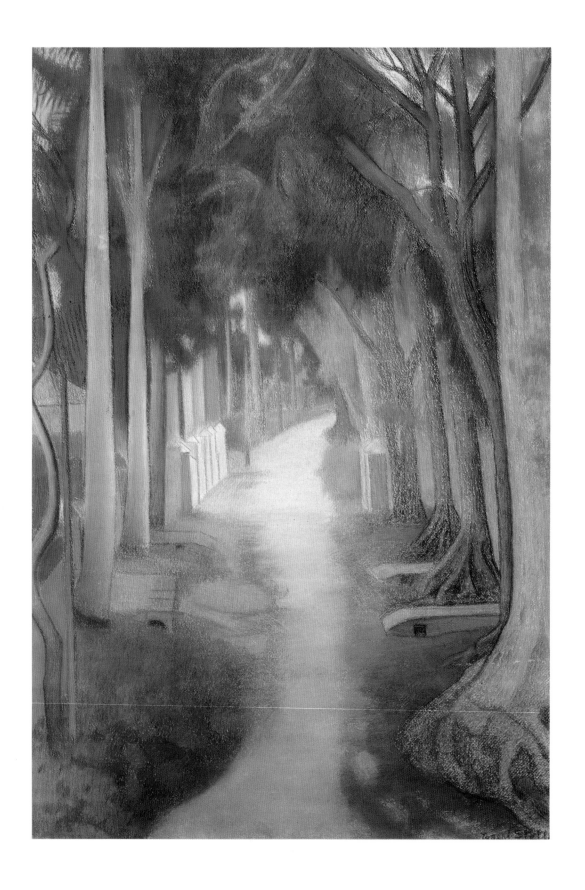

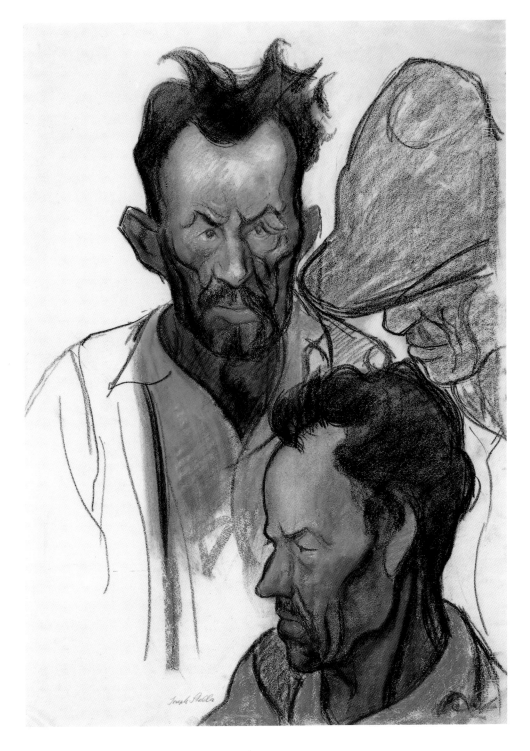

Figure 127

(opposite)
Path in Barbados,
ca. 1937–38
Pastel
37 x 26 in.
Private collection

Figure 128

Three Miners, ca. 1938
Pastel
26¼ x 18½ in.
Museum of Fine Arts,
Boston, Sophie M.
Friedman Fund

Figure 129

Portrait of Clara Fasano,
1943
Pastel
27⅛ x 15 in.
National Museum of
American Art,
Smithsonian Institution,
Washington, D.C.

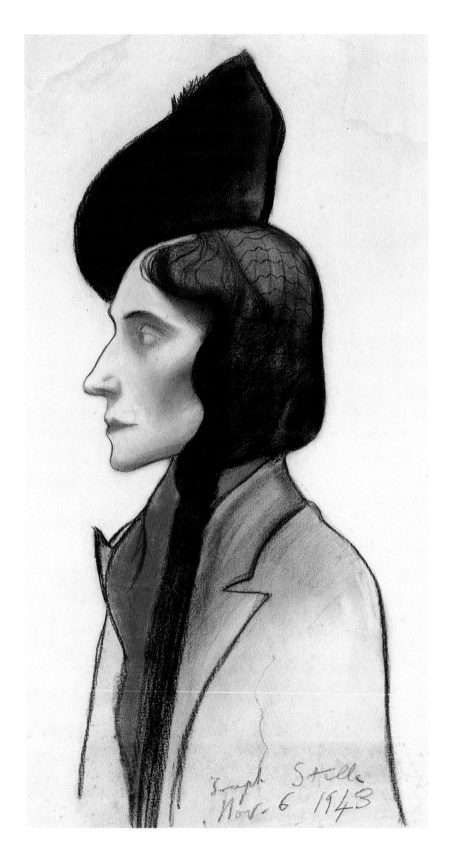

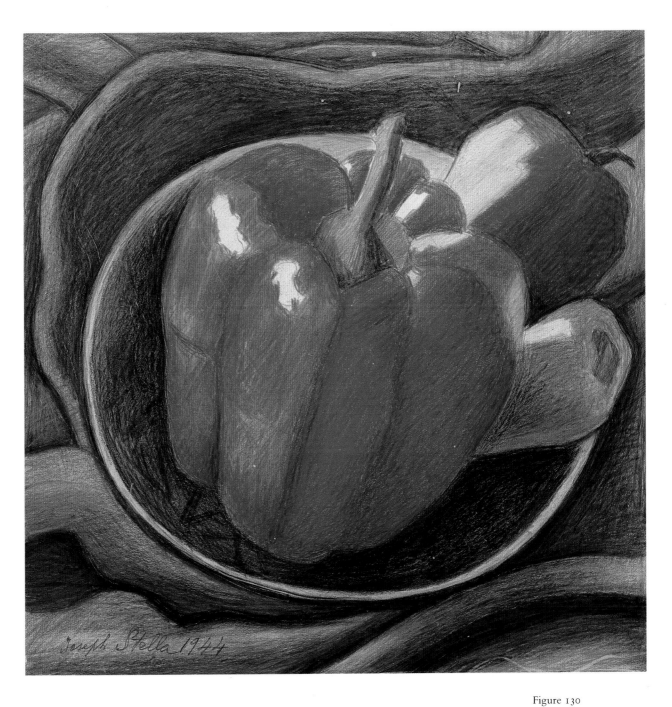

Figure 130

Red Pepper, 1944
Crayon and pencil
10¼ x 10¼ in.
James and Barbara
Palmer

trees receding regularly into the distance, bathed in a soft, glowing light, recalls the monumentality and rhythms of a classical basilica (see fig. 127).

The thread that ties together the diverse styles in which Stella worked during his career is the persistence of his romantic sensibility through which his modernist vision was filtered. Assimilating ideas and motifs from his study of poetry, music, and art, Stella integrated the many sources of his inspiration into a distinctive personal expression that continued to defy classification by movement or style. Stella's attempt to synthesize a contemporary expression that integrated significant elements of past traditions with bold, modernist innovations distinguishes him from the conservative academicians and studio artists as well as from many of the early modernist artists who broke with the art traditions of the past more completely and decisively.

In contrast to the rigid categories and absolute standards that had characterized the Victorian period, modernism allowed for contradiction, ambiguity, and diversity. Stella's identity as a modernist derives as much from his wholehearted acceptance of the attitude that favored an integrative approach to ideas as from his affiliation with a particular group, style, or movement.[122]

"Art's Poetic Gladiator"

After his return to the United States in 1935, Stella was no longer the prominent, financially successful artist who had left for Europe in 1926. Instead of enhancing his reputation as an internationally recognized artist, his nine years in Europe had removed him from the public eye. Urban realism and regionalism had come to dominate the artistic dialogue, related by their common focus on the American scene. Stella felt little empathy with either of these movements, and according to his dealer of that time, Bernard Rabin, he scorned the work created by artists associated with these two movements.[123]

The country was in the throes of the Great Depression, and Stella found it necessary to participate in a WPA easel project.[124] Most of the paintings he did on the project were variations on earlier themes, especially compositions based on *New York Interpreted* and his industrial subjects. The paintings done on his own relate strongly in theme and composition to *The Palm (Herons)* (see fig. 120). Unlike the urban and industrial subjects of his later years, the tropical subjects, his collages of the 1930s and 1940s, and his drawings of people, still lifes, and flower compositions sustain the vitality and originality that had characterized his earlier work. Out of the mainstream, however, his later work never attracted the attention or audience that his earlier work had.

A few perceptive critics maintained interest in Stella, but as Harry Salpeter recognized: "The man who breaks the mold takes a little longer to explain himself; those who have least trouble are the carbon copies."[125] His description of Stella as "art's poetic gladiator" conjures an image of a romantic Don Quixote in Sancho Panza's rotund body, tilting at the art establishment with brilliant palette and effulgent visions: "The boldness of his painting so effectively conceals the knowledge of the traditions of art Stella undoubtedly possesses that often he gives the impression of being more naive, more primitive than he really is."[126]

Joseph Stella's works on paper provide important clues to understanding his distinctive sensibility. They reveal an artist for whom technical mastery came early in his career, but who resisted the temptations of mere virtuosity. Considered as groups, by medium or subject matter, the drawings suggest concerns and sources shared by other artists of his generation that are less apparent in his paintings alone. Many of the drawings serve as a visual diary, albeit undated, of some of Stella's experiences that shaped his outlook and influenced his artistic expression. Moreover, they suggest some ideas that unite his seemingly disparate oeuvre. As a body of work, Stella's drawings disclose influences and interests that extended well beyond the Futurist compositions for which he is best known.

Stella's reputation as America's foremost Futurist painter has so dominated our perception of him that the rest of his work is often seen as little more than a footnote to his career. In fact, his Futurist-inspired paintings represent only one aspect of a large and varied body of work by an artist seeking freedom from all conventions and exploring myriad avenues of self-expression. Even in his most daring abstract compositions, such as *Battle of Light, Coney Island* and *Brooklyn Bridge*, the emotional, visionary quality of the expression is as essential to the work as the strictly formal dynamics of the composition.

The breadth of Joseph Stella's talent and interests is most apparent in his works on paper, which span the entire length of his career and far outnumber his paintings. Ranging from pencil, charcoal, crayon, and silverpoint drawings to pastel compositions, watercolors, and paper collages made from materials he found in the streets, many of Stella's drawings are finished works independent of his paintings. The drawings communicate, on a more intimate scale, his myriad inspirations and concerns. Even more dramatically than his paintings, they reveal the broad spectrum of styles and approaches that Stella explored throughout his career.

In a review of a recent exhibition of the artist's paintings and drawings on tropical subjects, Hilton Kramer wrote of "the other Stella," referring to an entire body of work that is not generally known.[127] In fact, there are several "other Stellas." Figure studies, portraits, flower drawings, collages, abstractions, still lifes, and landscapes in great quantity among his works on paper reveal an artist known only to a relatively small group of admirers. To appreciate the breadth of Stella's artistic vision, it is essential to look beyond the epic canvases to the lyric poetry and free verse of his drawings.

Notes

1. Irma B. Jaffe, *Joseph Stella* (Cambridge, Mass.: Harvard University Press, 1970), app. 1, no. 6, p. 7.

2. In an article on Joseph Stella, Carlo de Fornaro illustrates a drawing supposedly made by Stella at the age of twelve; see Carlo de Fornaro, "A Forceful Figure in American Art," *Arts and Decoration* 19 (August 1923): 60.

3. Carlo de Fornaro, "Joseph Stella: Outline of the Life, Work, and Times of a Great Master" (Unpublished manuscript, New York, 1939), p. 14.

4. The instructors at the Art Students League from October 1896 through May 1897 were J. Carroll Beckwith, Robert Blum, Charles Broughton, George DeForest Brush, Clifford Carleton, Kenyon Cox,

Mary T. Lawrence, H. Siddons Mowbray, Augustus Saint-Gaudens, J. H. Twachtman, Douglas Volk, and J. Alden Weir, but there is no record of whom Stella studied with.

5. Quoted in Jaffe, p. 11.

6. Although the exact dates and length of Stella's enrollment at the New York School of Art are unclear, it seems most likely that Stella studied at the school in 1898–99, soon after he left the Art Students League. Jaffe (p. 12) cites an exhibition of 1906 in which Stella is listed as a student of Chase's, but it seems likely that Stella was included as a former rather than a current student.

7. Stella, from "Notes about Joseph Stella," Joseph Stella Papers, Archives of American Art, Smithsonian Institution, roll 346: frame 1278 (hereafter cited as Stella Papers).

8. Ronald G. Pisano, *A Leading Spirit in American Art: William Merritt Chase, 1849–1916* (Seattle: Henry Art Gallery, 1983), pp. 88–89.

9. Fornaro, "Joseph Stella," p. 20.

10. Jaffe, p. 109.

11. Joseph Stella, "Discovery of America: Autobiographical Notes," *Art News* (November 1960 [written in 1946]): 42.

12. Joseph Stella, "The New Art," *The Trend* (June 1913): 393.

13. Stella, "Discovery," p. 42.

14. The subjects of the four remaining etchings are the head of a man wearing a cap, an old woman in a black veil reading a book, a profile of a woman facing right, and the lower portion of a tree trunk. Because of the strong similarity in pose, in reverse, of the boy playing a bagpipe to the boy in the composition dated 1909 (see fig. 11), one might assume that the etchings probably date from 1909–10 as well. The prints were not editioned in Stella's lifetime, but in 1961 Stella's agents Bernard Rabin and Nathan Krueger commissioned Emiliano Sironi of Pratt Institute to print restrikes from the original plates.

15. According to Fornaro, Stella had a large collection of reproductions of Italian Renaissance paintings. This drawing was reproduced in an article by Antonio Porpora ("Giuseppe Stella: Un pittore futurista di Basilicata a New York," *Italiani pel mondo* [September 1926]: 228) in which the sitter is identified as "Principessa E. Walser," referring to Helen Walser, the woman with whom Stella was living in the early 1920s. Although she signed her correspondence to Stella's patron Carl Weeks as Mrs. Stella, it is probable that she and Stella were not legally married.

16. Joseph Stella, "Autobiographical Notes," 1946, Stella Papers, roll 346: frame 1274.

17. Quoted in Jaffe, p. 91.

18. August Mosca to Jane Glaubinger in a letter dated 21 June 1983, as cited in Jane Glaubinger, "Two Drawings by Joseph Stella," *Bulletin of the Cleveland Museum of Art* 70, no. 10 (December 1983): 391–92.

19. According to a manuscript sent to Nathan Krueger on 10 October 1961, Stella often used silverpoint for the underdrawing of his paintings because it did not smear like charcoal or pencil; see August Mosca, August Mosca Papers, Archives of American Art, Smithsonian Institution, roll N70–77 (hereafter cited as Mosca Papers).

20. The portrait of Joe Gould in the Museum of Modern Art (see fig. 20) was originally identified as a portrait of Louis Michael Eilshemius. Although there is a strong resemblance between the two faces, especially the wire-rimmed glasses and goatee, comparison with the Hirshhorn portrait of Eilshemius (see fig. 21) shows a difference in the shape of the eyebrows and style of the hair. Furthermore, the MOMA portrait closely resembles a portrait of Gould in the collection of one of Stella's relatives as well as a portrait of him by Stella reproduced in *Broom* 5, no. 3 (October 1923): 144.

21. According to Pliny, this proverb actually originated with Apelles; see Jaffe, p. viii.

22. Helen Walser was a woman with whom Stella lived for approximately five years in the early 1920s. According to uncatalogued letters given to the Archives of American Art in 1986, the artist reinitiated contact with her in 1943 after having received her address from Stefi Kiesler in a letter dated 29 December 1942. (By that time she had married a man named Bill Richardson and lived in Brewster, New York.) The painting based on this composition (*Profile*, Hirshhorn Museum and Sculpture Garden) is inscribed on the verso, "painted in 1940," and seems to be a nostalgic remembrance of a happier time. At this time, Stella was still upset by the death of his wife, Mary French, in Barbados in November 1939. Although he had not lived with her much of his life, Stella had accompanied her to Barbados in 1937, sent her money, and corresponded with her until her death.

23. *Amazon* (see fig. 23), one of Stella's better-known paintings, repeats very closely the pose, feature, and size of the silverpoint drawing of Kathleen Millay, even though this painting was later identified as a portrait of Edna St. Vincent Millay (ACA Gallery catalogue, cover illustration, summer 1971).

24. Although Stella did many drawings of the Brooklyn Bridge, no direct studies for the 1919 painting of the bridge have been identified. One drawing that has been published and exhibited as a study for this painting seems to be a drawing over a photograph of the painting; see *The Société Anonyme and the Dreier Bequest at Yale University: A Catalogue Raisonné* (New Haven, Conn., and London: Yale University Press, 1984), p. 633.

25. Quoted in Jaffe, p. 78.

26. Stella, "Discovery," p. 41.

27. Fornaro, "Joseph Stella," p. 5.

28. Stella, "Discovery," p. 41.

29. Because none of these drawings has been located, their medium and size cannot be determined.

30. The magazine was also known as *Charities and Commons* until April 1909, but it is listed in the Library of Congress *Union List of Serials* (third edition) as *Survey* from December 1897 through May 1952.

31. Stella, "Discovery," pp. 41–42.

32. Fornaro, "Joseph Stella," p. 4.

33. Stella, "Discovery," p. 42.

34. Drawings from "The Pittsburgh Survey" also appeared in Mary Antin, "They Who Knock at Our Gate," *American Magazine* (18 April 1914): 18–24, and Antonio Stella, *Some Aspects of Italian Immigration to the United States* (New York and London: Putnam, 1924).

35. *The Survey* 36 (6 May 1916): 154. The drawing is entitled "From the Campagna," and the legend printed beneath it reads: "A young Italian girl, who, with two other children, has been brought by the mother to this country following the death of the father. An uncle living in America meets them and puts up a bond that they will be given proper schooling."

36. Stella, "The New Art," p. 393.

37. Stella, from "Notes about Stella," Stella Papers, frame 1279.

38. *Chimneys, Pittsburgh* was published in *The Survey (Charities and Commons)* 21 (2 January 1909): 515 on the same page as a poem by Richard Realf entitled *Hymn of Pittsburgh*, which might be considered an alternate title for this drawing.

39. Quoted in Jaffe, p. 21.

40. The reference numbers assigned to these Whistler etchings by Edward G. Kennedy, in *The Etched Work of Whistler* (New York: Grolier Club, 1910), are as follows: *Street at Sauverne* (K.19), *The Kitchen* (K.24), *Old Battersea Bridge* (K.177), *Old Putney Bridge* (K.178), *Nocturne: Palaces* (K.202), and *Nocturne, Furnace* (K.213).

41. In a recent examination, Boston Museum of Fine Arts paper conservator Elizabeth Lunning observed five heavily incised lines applied with a hard, single-pointed tool on top of the pastel. She also noted that the paper is exceptionally smooth for a pastel drawing, which needs tooth to pull the pastel off the stick and hold it on the paper. Such observations suggest that this drawing may have been done on a prepared paper, which would have provided the necessary tooth for the pastel, and that the incised lines may have been made with a metalpoint tool. Lunning's findings are documented in a memo to Marilyn Symmes, curator of graphic arts, the Toledo Museum of Art, 29 April 1989.

42. The concise and perceptive analysis of Tonalism by Wanda M. Corn, in *The Color of Mood: American Tonalism, 1880–1910* (San Francisco: M. H. De Young Memorial Museum and the California Palace of the Legion of Honor, 1972), was the source for my description of this movement.

43. Mosca Papers, p. 3 of a manuscript sent to Nathan Krueger on 10 October 1961.

44. This exhibition was held from 4–25 January 1908 and included paintings by such artists as Robert Henri, George Luks, William Glackens, Childe Hassam, Leon Dabo, John Sloan, and William Merritt Chase among others. The exhibition received abundant attention in the press because it was the first time that photographs had been shown simultaneously with paintings and because vandalism done to a painting by Van Deering Perrine attracted popular interest. William Sharpe, in "New York, Night, and Cultural Mythmaking: The Nocturne in Photography, 1900–1925," *Smithsonian Studies in American Art* (Fall 1988): 3–21, emphasizes the importance of the nocturne for pictorialist photographers.

45. Stella, "Discovery," p. 64.

46. Stella, "The New Art," pp. 394–95.

47. Quoted in Jaffe, p. 38.

48. Wanda Corn, "In Detail: Joseph Stella and *New York Interpreted*," *Portfolio* 4, no. 1 (January–February 1982): 40.

49. Joshua Taylor, *Futurism* (New York: Museum of Modern Art, 1961), p. 13.

50. In particular, these ideas were expressed in the "Initial Manifesto of Futurism," first published in *Le Figaro*, Paris, 20 February 1909, and "The Exhibitors to the Public," first published in French for the exhibition at Bernheim-Jeune, Paris, 5–12 February 1912. For English translations of these documents, see Taylor, *Futurism*, pp. 124–25, 127–29.

51. Stella, "The New Art," p. 395.

52. Fornaro, p. 34.

53. Joseph Stella, "The Brooklyn Bridge (A Page of My Life)," *transition*, no. 16–17 (June 1929): 86.

54. See Sandra Gail Levin, "Wassily Kandinsky and the American Avant-Garde, 1912-1950" (Ph.D. diss., Rutgers University, 1976), p. 45. Levin focuses on the reception of Kandinsky's art and ideas within the Stieglitz circle, but Stella's association with artists in this group, while he was not actually part of it, suggests that he was also familiar with Kandinsky.

55. Stella, "The Brooklyn Bridge," p. 88.

56. Charles John Kostelnick, "Gothic Views, Romantic Visions: The Spatial Dynamics of Modern Art and Literature" (Ph.D. diss., University of Illinois at Champaign-Urbana, 1981), p. 354.

57. Fornaro, "Joseph Stella," p. 1.

58. Charmion Von Wiegand, "Joseph Stella, Painter of Brooklyn Bridge" (unpublished essay), p. 8. Stella also quoted extensively from Dante and Shakespeare. Carlo de Fornaro cites Stella's regard for the English poet Shelley, and Stella acknowledged his admiration for Thoreau as one of "the three giants, towering in the American Olympus of Literature" along with Poe and Whitman; see Stella, "For the American Painting," in *Stella* (New York: A.C.A. Gallery, 1943).

59. Stella, "Discovery of America," p. 65.

60. See Alice O'Mara Piron, "Urban Metaphor in American Art and Literature, 1910–1930" (Ph.D. diss., Northwestern University, 1982), p. 9.

61. Stella, "The Brooklyn Bridge," p. 87. Theosophists and psychic researchers used the telegraph pole as an analogy for mental telepathy, because it required an invisible field of force to overcome finite, physical limitations.

62. Piron, p. 43.

63. Stella, "For the American Painting," no page.

64. Stella's second group of industrial subjects dates from approximately 1917 to 1921. See Jaffe, pp. 58–61, for an explanation of the difficulties in dating these works precisely.

65. Stella, "The Brooklyn Bridge," pp. 86–87.

66. "Bethlehem: Not of the Shepherds but of the Steelmakers, As Sketched by Joseph Stella," The Survey 41 (1 February 1919); "Makers of Wings: Monotypes by Joseph Stella," The Survey 41 (1 March 1919). Although the drawings for "The Coal By-Product Oven," The Survey 51 (1 March 1924) were not published until six years later, they were almost certainly done between 1918 and 1920. A newspaper photograph of a swan among some uncatalogued Stella papers at the Archives of American Art suggests that he may have used photographs as the source of his imagery more frequently than has been supposed.

67. The term Cubist-Realism was first used by Milton W. Brown in "Cubist-Realism: An American Style," Marsayas 3 (1946): 139–60, a seminal article on which subsequent discussions of Precisionism are based.

68. Stella, from "Notes about Stella," Stella Papers, frame 1279. These notes are written in the third person, but it is apparent from the autobiographical content that they were written by Stella himself.

69. Collage #4: Bookman (1920–22; Hirshhorn Museum and Sculpture Garden) and Study for Skyscraper (whereabouts unknown) were reproduced in the special "Stella Number," The Little Review 9, no. 3 (Autumn 1922).

70. August Mosca, an artist who spent a good deal of time with Stella in the late 1930s and early 1940s, remembers Stella picking up interesting bits of paper and debris as they walked through the streets. Stella gave him some of the collages he made, but he did not discuss the meaning of the collages with Mosca (interview by author with August Mosca, Shelter Island, New York, 3 September 1988).

71. August Mosca remembers that Stella referred to the collages as naturelles (Mosca Papers, p. 8). In a letter to the author (15 January 1987), Andrew Crispo, who purchased many of the collages from Mosca, suggests that Mosca referred to them as macchina naturale, a term Crispo adopted. He numbered them successively as he acquired them. Hence, the numbers have no relation to the dates or order in which they were made, as is also true of works titled simply with numbers by other art dealers. Macchina naturale #29 has the words macchie naturali written over the artist's signature, but this seems to be the only written reference to this designation.

72. See "Americans in the Rough: Character Studies at Ellis Island," The Outlook, 23 December 1905.

73. This scrap is from the upper-left corner of p. 98 of Roger Fry, "Mantegna As a Mystic," Burlington Magazine 33 (December 1905): 87–98. The collage almost certainly dates from several decades later, suggesting that either the article may have been one that Stella had kept for many years or found in a used bookshop.

74. See Charles C. Eldredge, American Imagination and Symbolist Painting (New York: Grey Art Gallery and Study Center, New York University, 1979).

75. Charles Eldredge, "Nature Symbolized: American Painting from Ryder to Hartley," in *The Spiritual in Art: Abstract Painting, 1890–1985* (Los Angeles: Los Angeles County Museum of Art, 1986).

76. Stella, "The New Art," p. 394.

77. Stella, "Discovery," p. 65.

78. Françoise Meltzer, in "Color As Cognition in Symbolist Verse," *Critical Inquiry* 5, no. 2 (Winter 1978): 253–73, provides an excellent discussion of this subject, which she summarizes as: "color is not only a component vital to symbolist semiology but to its epistemological assumptions as well."

79. Stella, "The Brooklyn Bridge," p. 87.

80. According to August Mosca, Stella used Nupastel, a set of forty-three hard pastels, which he liked for their spareness. Occasionally, he used the German Mengs for a softer impasto effect. He worked directly on the spot, without preparatory sketches, on a variety of textured papers, including Michelet, Strathmore, and his favorite, the French Canson-Montgolfier (interview by author with August Mosca, Shelter Island, New York, 3 September 1988).

81. Quoted in Jaffe, p. 84.

82. Two blue flowers and a small, curved tendril, arranged vertically in the center of the halolike circles, resemble a figure of the Virgin when seen at a normal distance for viewing this large painting. Ruth Bohan has noted the resemblance of this motif to the Virgin in a tree in a painting by the Italian Symbolist Giovanni Segantini, *L'angelo della vita* (1894; Civica Galleria d'Arte Moderna, Milan), and has suggested that its title may have been a source for Stella's title *Tree of My Life*. An even closer resemblance exists with Gustave Moreau's *Mystic Flower* (ca. 1875; Musée Gustave Moreau, Paris), in which the Virgin grows out of an enormous lily, watered by the blood of martyrs.

83. Meltzer, p. 260, outlines the following characteristics of *poésie pure*: hermeticism, linguistic distortion, abstractionism, and musicality.

84. Quoted in Jaffe, pp. 9, 106.

85. Quoted ibid., p. 26.

86. This interpretation of the Middle Ages was widely held among liberal American artists who read *The Education of Henry Adams*, published in 1906. A corollary to this idea was that the Italian Renaissance marked the decline of spiritual values, a belief that contradicted Stella's own admiration for Italian Renaissance art. It is clear that he admired the spiritual qualities of Giotto, Piero della Francesca, Tintoretto, and other Italian Renaissance artists (see Jaffe, pp. 154–55, 164–65).

87. Kostelnick, p. 347.

88. The reference to the Eiffel Tower is even more pronounced in the painting that seems to have been based on this drawing, *Brooklyn Bridge: Variation on an Old Theme* (1939; Whitney Museum of American Art), in which a view of New York is placed underneath the rounded arch at the bottom of the composition, similar to the view of Paris that is visible beneath the arch at the base of the Eiffel Tower.

89. Quoted in Jaffe, p. 75.

90. From a letter of Joseph Stella in the Newark Museum files, 1944, as quoted in *American Art in the Newark Museum: Paintings, Drawings and Sculpture* (Newark, N.J.: Newark Museum, 1981), p. 42.

91. Meltzer, p. 259. The word may have had additional meaning for Stella, because the Italian word for "swan," one of his favorite subjects, is *cigno*.

92. It is often impossible to distinguish the difference between an oxidized silverpoint line and one made with a goldpoint, even with a microscope or a highly trained eye.

93. Three very similar versions of the same subject have been found. All are pastel on paper of a similar size and distinguished

primarily by the handling of the background, suggesting that this motif was important for Stella.

94. In a painting of a single lotus blossom (*Lotus Flower*, oil on glass, collection of Dr. and Mrs. Martin Weissman), Stella simultaneously depicted an internal and external view of the flower showing a golden seedpod encased in a womblike form surrounded by protective petals. Ella M. Foshay, in *Reflections of Nature* (New York: Alfred A. Knopf, 1984), p. 71, suggests that Stella's unusual view was influenced by Max von Laue's discovery of the X-ray in 1912. In his many drawings of the lotus flower, Stella's penetration of its external appearance is implicit rather than explicit, spiritual rather than physical.

95. Stella, "Discovery," p. 66.

96. This composition represents a rare example of two almost identical drawings by Stella. Only minor differences distinguish this drawing (see fig. 118) from the drawing in the collection of the Metropolitan Museum of Art (53.45.3).

97. Stella, "Discovery," p. 65.

98. Joseph Stella, "On Painting," *Broom* 1, no. 2 (December 1921): 122.

99. Fornaro, "Joseph Stella," p. 1. This theme frequently recurred in Italian Renaissance paintings of Francis of Assisi, the saint with whom Stella seemed to identify most closely in his writings.

100. Stella Papers, frame 1245.

101. Jaffe, p. 183, suggests that this title relates to Stella's friendship with Amedeo Modigliani, who was always speaking about doing a painting called *Il canto del cigno* (Song of the Nightingale). It may also refer to a Rumanian legend of the rosebush, in which one huge bud gave birth to a handsome prince. When the prince grew up, he wished to return to the tranquility of his infancy and serve others through beauty. He searched for the rosebush that bore him, and a nightingale sang a dirge over the spot where the rose-

bush had stood. The nightingale stayed until he had sung the soul of the prince back into a rose. The prince cast himself upon the spot where he had been born, and the bird continued to sing more loudly and more sweetly. Roots began to extend from the prince's limbs, and at dawn, he was transformed into a rose tree (see Charles M. Skinner, *Myths and Legends of Flowers, Trees, Fruits, and Plants* [1911; reprint, Philadelphia and London: J. B. Lippincott Company, 1925], pp. 234–35).

102. For an interesting discussion of the musical structure of this painting, see Corn, "In Detail," pp. 43–44.

103. Whistler, letter to *The World*, 22 May 1878, reprinted in *The Gentle Art of Making Enemies* (1890; reprint, New York: Dover, 1967), pp. 127–28.

104. For an excellent discussion of synesthesia and related beliefs, see Judith Zilczer, " 'Color Music': Synaesthesia and Nineteenth-Century Sources for Abstract Art," *Artibus et historiae* 16 (1987): 101–26.

105. Stella's composition is related to a photograph by Man Ray of a flower and an egg (illustrated in *Photographs by Man Ray: 105 Works, 1920–1934* [New York: Dover, 1979], p. 20), an image which Man Ray later transformed into an even more conspicuously birdlike form in an allegorical self-portrait, *The Misunderstood One* (1938; whereabouts unknown).

106. Jack Flam, *Matisse: The Man and His Art, 1869–1918* (Ithaca, N.Y., and London: Cornell University Press, 1986), p. 173. It is possible that Stella saw the goldfish paintings in Matisse's studio in the spring of 1912, before he left Paris.

107. Ibid., pp. 343, 500 n. 37.

108. See John F. Moffitt, "Marcel Duchamp: Alchemist of the Avant-Garde," in *The Spiritual in Art*, p. 264.

109. Francis Naumann, "Cryptography and the Arensberg Circle," *Arts Magazine* 51, no. 9 (May 1977): 127–33.

110. A famous photograph of Stella and Duchamp taken by Man Ray, with his own presence indicated by a photograph of himself on the wall, documents their close friendship. A photograph by Man Ray of Stella holding a guitar at a Paris café table (see chronology), probably taken between 1926 and 1933, suggests that Stella maintained this friendship well after the Arensberg circle dissolved.

111. Quoted in Margery Rex, " 'Dada' Will Get You If You Don't Watch Out: It Is on the Way Here," *New York Evening Journal*, 29 January 1921, reprinted in *New York Dada*, ed. Rudolf E. Kuenzli (New York: Willis Locker and Owens, 1986), p. 140.

112. Stella, "My Sermon about Christ," quoted in Jaffe, p. 50.

113. Stella's relationship to Duchamp and the connection between Stella's glass paintings and Duchamp's *Large Glass* are discussed in great detail in Ruth Bohan, "Joseph Stella's *Man in Elevated (Train)*," in *Dada/Dimensions*, ed. Stephen C. Foster (Ann Arbor, Mich.: UMI Research Press, 1985), pp. 187–219.

114. See Joshua C. Taylor, *The Graphic Work of Umberto Boccioni* (New York: Museum of Modern Art, 1961), nos. 138, 220–26. All but the first of these drawings were done in 1912, possibly while Boccioni was in Paris for the Futurist exhibition at Bernheim-Jeune. In "Discovery," p. 64, Stella implies that he met the Futurist artists, including Boccioni, and visited their studios, which were located near his own. Although he seems to have exaggerated his contact with the Futurists at that time, it is quite possible that he saw Boccioni's drawings at his studio. The shape of the light in another of Stella's glass paintings (*Untitled*, Whitney Museum of American Art) also recalls the triangular light fixture in one of Boccioni's drawings (no. 224).

115. Hartley was at the New York School of Art from fall 1899 through the end of the school year, when Stella also attended that school, but it is not known whether or not the two students knew each other at the time.

116. One of the most cogent discussions of the importance of symbolism for American modernism appears in Charles Eldredge, "Nature Symbolized," pp. 113–29. Stella is not discussed, possibly because he was not a member of the Stieglitz circle.

117. There is no evidence of direct contact with these artists until Stella began to frequent the Arensberg salon that Charles Demuth, Arthur Dove, and Marsden Hartley also attended. The humorous article "Pug Debs Make Society Bow," *New York Dada* 1 (April 1921) featured Stella and Hartley, suggesting that the two were at least acquaintances, if not friends.

118. Louise Varèse mentions that Stella's name appeared on the letterhead for the International Composers' Guild, but she does not indicate what Stella actually did (Louise Varèse, *A Looking-glass Diary* [New York: W. W. Norton and Company, 1972], p. 165).

119. Georgette Leblanc was the mistress of the Symbolist poet Maurice Maeterlinck. Her performance featured *Vocalize Byzantine* by George Antheil, Poldowsky's *Cortège*, Ravel's *Shéhérazade* and *Chanson Espagnole*, pieces by Borodin, Rimsky-Korsakov, Rudhyar, and Whithorne as well as Chinese poems. The title of the evening's "programme exotique" suggests that it may have been conceived as a musical interpretation of Stella's painting *Tree of My Life* (I would like to thank Noel Frackman for directing me to a copy of this program in the John Storrs Papers, Archives of American Art, Smithsonian Institution, Box 10, Folder: Memorabilia).

120. There was some crossover from the Stieglitz group, and Stieglitz himself visited the Arensbergs on occasion. Among the artists who frequented the Arensberg apartment were Duchamp, Picabia, Gleizes, Crotti, Varèse, Demuth, Dove, Hartley, Man Ray, John Covert, Charles Sheeler, Morton Schamberg, and Louis Eilshemius.

The poets Henri-Martin Barzun, Alfred Kreymborg, Amy Lowell, Allan Norton, William Carlos Williams, and Wallace Stevens, as well as the composer Edgard Varèse, the critic Henri-Pierre Roche, the dancer Isadora Duncan, the editor Max Eastman, and others were also members of the group.

121. These include the silverpoint portrait of Marcel Duchamp (ca. 1920; Museum of Modern Art), the *Goldfish* pastel (see fig. 124), a watercolor study (whereabouts unknown) related to *Spring* (ca. 1914–16) and *Battle of Lights* (ca. 1913; both Yale University Art Gallery), and two drawings given to the Metropolitan Museum (*Single Flower* [1919], and *Landscape* [see fig. 88]); see *The Société Anonyme and the Dreier Bequest at Yale University*, p. 772.

122. This definition of modernism is developed in Daniel Joseph Singal, "Toward a Definition of American Modernism," *American Quarterly* 39, no. 1, (Spring 1987): 7–26.

123. Interview by author with Bernard Rabin, Newark, New Jersey, 17 July 1986.

124. Civilian personnel records of the General Services Administration indicate that Stella began working on a WPA project on 3 September 1935 at a salary of $103.40 per month, that his pay was reduced to $95.44 per month on 25 May 1936, and that he was terminated on 17 August 1939. Jacob Kainen remembers Stella's bitter comment, made while both were waiting in line for a WPA check, that he (Stella), an artist who had been in the Armory Show, was now forced to stand in line at the New York Armory for a government check (interview by author with Jacob Kainen, Washington, D.C., 2 July 1986).

125. Harry Salpeter, "Stella: Art's Poetic Gladiator," *Esquire,* July 1941, p. 92.

126. Ibid.

127. Hilton Kramer, "The Other Stella," *Art and Antiques* (January 1989): 97.

May Ray, *Portrait of Joseph Stella,* ca. 1926–33, silver print. Copyright ARS N.Y./The Man Ray Trust, Paris, 1990.

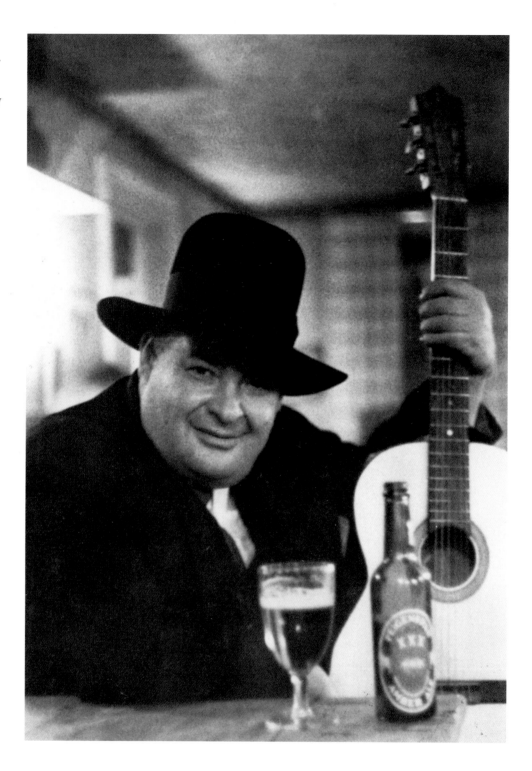

CHRONOLOGY

1877	Born in Muro Lucano, Italy, June 13.
1896	Arrives in New York, March 1.
1896–97	Studies medicine and pharmacology.
1897	Studies at Art Students League, November–December.
1898–1900	Attends New York School of Art and studies under William Merritt Chase.
1900–1905	Lives in Bowery area of Lower East Side.
1901	Studies with Chase at his summer school, Shinnecock, Long Island.
1902	Reputedly marries Mary Geraldine Walter French.

1905	Publishes seven drawings of immigrants in *Outlook*, December.
1906	Illustrates Ernest Poole's novel *The Voice of the Street*.
1907	Goes to West Virginia to record Monongah mine disaster; six drawings published in *The Survey*, December.
1908	Draws workers and steel mills in Pittsburgh; results appear in January, February, and March 1909 issues of *The Survey*.
1909–10	Returns to Europe; spends first year in Italy, mostly in Rome, Florence, and Muro Lucano.
	Befriends the artist Antonio Mancini in Rome.
1910	Has solo exhibition of drawings, Carnegie Institute, Pittsburgh; also shown in Chicago and New York.
1911–12	Lives in Paris and meets Matisse, Modigliani, Carra, and possibly Boccioni and Severini, among other avant-garde artists.
1912	Sees Futurist exhibition, Galerie Bernheim-Jeune, Paris, February.
	Exhibits three works, Salon des Indépendants, Paris, March–May.
	Travels briefly to Italy before returning to New York in December.
1913	Participates in International Exhibition of Modern Art (The Armory Show), New York, February–March.
	Has first solo exhibition of paintings, Italian National Club, New York.
	Publishes "The New Art" in *The Trend*, June.
1914	Participates in exhibition of modern art, Montross Gallery, New York, where *Battle of Lights, Coney Island* is first shown.
1915	Meets Duchamp, Picabia, Varèse, and other artists, musicians, and writers at the salon hosted by Walter and Louise Arensberg at their New York apartment.
1916–17	Moves to Brooklyn, where he teaches Italian at a Baptist seminary in the Williamsburg section.
1918	Travels to Pittsburgh and Bethlehem, Pennsylvania, to produce illustrations of the war effort for *The Survey*.
1919	Exhibits first major industrial paintings, Bourgeois Galleries, New York.
	Paints *Tree of My Life* and *Brooklyn Bridge*.
1920	Has retrospective exhibition, Bourgeois Galleries, March–April.
	Joins Société Anonyme and participates in their exhibitions throughout the decade.
1920–22	Paints *The Voice of the City of New York Interpreted*.
1920–25	Lives in New York with Helen Walser, her son, and her daughter.
1921	Publishes "On Painting" in *Broom*, December.
1922	Issue of *The Little Review*, autumn, devoted to Stella.
	Participates in *Salon Dada, Exposition Internationale,* Galerie Montaigne,

	Paris, 6–30 June.
	Travels to Naples and visits Pompeii, Herculaneum, Paestum, and Capri.
1923	Returns to New York.
	New York Interpreted included in inaugural exhibition of Société Anonyme, January.
	Becomes a United States citizen, 30 August.
1924	Has solo exhibition, Dudensing Gallery, New York.
1925	Visits patron Carl Weeks in Des Moines, August (Stella's only documented trip in the United States outside the New York–New Jersey area).
1926	Has solo exhibitions, New Gallery and Valentine Gallery, New York (also in 1928, 1931, 1935).
	Has painting exhibition, City Library Gallery, Des Moines Association of Fine Arts, May.
	Travels to Europe, visits Naples and probably North Africa.
1926–27	Returns to New York.
1928	Returns to Europe, first to Paris.
1929	Travels to Naples, also probably visits North Africa, January–June. Returns to Paris and probably visits Riviera.
	Has solo exhibition, Angiporto Galleria, Naples.
	"Confession" published in *The Little Review*, spring. "The Brooklyn Bridge (A Page of My Life)," published in *transition*, June, after appearing as a privately printed and distributed brochure.
1930–34	Lives in Paris, return visit to Italy probable.
1930	Has solo exhibition, Galerie Sloden, Paris, May.
	Visits North Africa, including Biskra and Chad.
1932	Has solo exhibition, Washington Palace, Paris.
1934	Visits Rome for *International Exhibition of Religious Art*, in which he exhibits twelve paintings.
1935	Has final solo exhibition at Valentine Gallery, January.
	Returns to New York and lives in the Bronx with Mary French Stella.
	Works intermittently on WPA Federal Art Project through August 1939.
1937	Has solo exhibition, Cooperative Gallery (later called Rabin and Kruger), Newark, N.J., December.
	Travels to Barbados with Mary French Stella, where he stays for several months.
1938	Leaves Barbados for Europe; visits Paris, Venice, and Naples.
	Returns to New York by December.
1939	Has retrospective exhibition, Newark Museum, April.
	Mary French Stella dies in Barbados, 29 November.
1940	Develops heart disease.

1941	Has solo exhibition, Associated American Artists, New York.
1942	Has solo exhibition, M. Knoedler and Company, New York, April–May. Illness forces him to give up his studio; relies heavily on nephew Sergio Stella for care.
1943	Develops thrombosis in left eye. "For the American Painting" is published in catalogue for his exhibition at A.C.A. Gallery, New York, November.
1945	Suffers serious fall while serving on exhibition jury for Portrait of America Show.
1946	Dies of heart attack, 5 November.
1958	Solo exhibition at Zabriskie Gallery, New York, April–May (also 1959, 1960, 1961 [collages]).
1960	Solo exhibition of drawings at Museum of Modern Art, New York, October–November; circulated to fifteen cities. "Discovery of America: Autobiographical Notes," published in *Art News,* November (written in 1946).
1963	Two exhibitions at Robert Schoelkopf Gallery, New York, January and October–November (also 1964, 1977, 1979, 1981, 1984). Exhibition at Drew University, Madison, N.J., February–March. Retrospective at Whitney Museum of American Art, New York, November–December. Exhibition at Harry Salpeter Gallery, New York, November.
1964	Exhibition at Storm King Art Center, Mountainville, N.Y. Exhibition at Seton Hall University, South Orange, N.J., November–December.
1966–67	Exhibition at Galleria Astrolabio Arte, Rome, December–January.
1968	Exhibition at University of Maryland Art Gallery, College Park, September–October.
1978	Exhibition at Donald Morris Gallery, Birmingham, Mich. (also 1982).
1983	Exhibition of thirty-four works from Hirshhorn Museum and Sculpture Garden collection in Washington, D.C., May–July, and at Columbus Museum of Art, Ohio, February–March 1984.
1988	Exhibition of works on tropical subjects at Richard York Gallery, New York, October.

SELECT BIBLIOGRAPHY

Extensive bibliographies on Joseph Stella appear in Jaffe's *Joseph Stella* and in the works by Baur and Zilczer, listed below. This bibliography is complete for publications since 1983 and includes several items not cited in previous bibliographies.

Baker, Elizabeth C. "The Consistent Inconsistency of Joseph Stella." *Art News* 62 (December 1963): 47, 62–63.

Baur, John I. H. *Joseph Stella*. New York: Praeger Publishers, 1971.

Bohan, Ruth. "Joseph Stella's *Man in Elevated (Train)*." In *Dada/Dimensions*, edited by Stephen C. Foster. Ann Arbor, Mich.: UMI Research Press, 1985.

Cassidy, Donna M. "The Painted Music of America in the Works of Arthur G. Dove, John Marin, and Joseph Stella."

Ph.D. diss., Boston University, 1987.

Cate, Phillips Dennis. *Paintings and Drawings by Joseph Stella from New Jersey Collections.* New Brunswick, N.J.: Rutgers University Art Gallery, 1970.

De Fornaro, Carlo. "A Forceful Figure in American Art." *Arts and Decoration* 19 (August 1923): 17, 60–61.

Foley, Kathy K. "Joseph Stella: Enigmatic Painter." *Dayton Art Institute Bulletin* 36, no. 1 (October 1977): 4–11.

Glaubinger, Jane. "Two Drawings by Joseph Stella." *Cleveland Museum of Art Bulletin* 70, no. 10 (December 1983): 82–395.

Jaffe, Irma B. *Joseph Stella.* Cambridge, Mass.: Harvard University Press, 1970.

———. *Joseph Stella: The Tropics.* New York: Richard York Gallery, 1988.

———. "Forum: Joseph Stella's Study for 'New York Interpreted.'" *Drawing* 10, no. 6 (March–April 1989).

Knox, George. "Crane and Stella: Conjunction of Painterly and Poetic Worlds." In *Texas Studies in Literature and Language* 12 (Winter 1971): 689–707.

Kramer, Hilton. "The Other Stella." *Art and Antiques* (January 1989).

Mott, Eileen McCarthy. "Joseph Stella: An Evaluation of Style." Master's thesis, University of Maryland, 1978.

Weber, Bruce. *The Fine Line: Drawing with Silver in America.* West Palm Beach, Fla.: The Norton Gallery and School of Art, 1986.

Zilczer, Judith. *Joseph Stella: The Hirshhorn Museum and Sculpture Garden Collection.* Washington, D.C.: Smithsonian Institution Press, 1983.

INDEX